Quantum L

"Creation, resurrection, afterlife, the problem of pain, ... meaning, the nature of reality — I cannot think of a meta-question that this book omits. And I cannot think of a more trustworthy guide than John Polkinghorne, who holds up both ends of the science/faith debate."
– **Philip Yancey**

"Here is the revealing story of an influential Christian and brilliant physicist whose life trajectory has been astonishingly unexpected. Written with sensitivity and clarity, this extraordinary spiritual biography of Revd John Polkinghorne illuminates one of the leading figures in our contemporary science and religion dialogue."
– **Dr Owen Gingerich, Harvard-Smithsonian Center for Astrophysics, and author of *God's Universe***

"A very accessible guide to the life and thought of this leading thinker. Immensely worthwhile reading for anyone concerned with the relation of faith and science."
– **Alister E. McGrath, Professor of Theology, Ministry and Education, King's College, London**

"An interesting and perceptive study of the life of a great and thoughtful person, who emphasized the relation between science and religion."
– **Charles Townes, winner of the Nobel Prize for Physics, and Professor of Physics, University of California**

Quantum Leap

How John Polkinghorne Found God in Science and Religion

Dean Nelson
and Karl Giberson

MONARCH
BOOKS
Oxford, UK & Grand Rapids, Michigan, USA

First published in the UK in 2011 by Monarch Books
(a publishing imprint of Lion Hudson plc)
Wilkinson House, Jordan Hill Road, Oxford OX2 8DR, England
Tel: +44 (0)1865 302750 Fax: +44 (0)1865 302757
Email: monarch@lionhudson.com
www.lionhudson.com

ISBN 978 1 85424 972 2 (UK print)
ISBN 978 0 7459 5401 1(US print)
ISBN 978 0 85721 128 6 (epub)
ISBN 978 0 85721 127 9 (Kindle)
ISBN 978 0 85721 129 3 (PDF)

Distributed by:
UK: Marston Book Services, PO Box 269, Abingdon, Oxon, OX14 4YN
USA: Trafalgar Square Publishing, 814 N Franklin Street, Chicago, IL 60610

Acknowledgments

Unless otherwise stated, Scripture quotations taken from the Holy Bible, New International Version, copyright © 1973, 1978, 1984 by the International Bible Society. Used by permission of Zondervan and Hodder & Stoughton Limited. All rights reserved. The "NIV" and "New International Version" trademarks are registered in the United States Patent and Trademark Office by International Bible Society. Use of either trademark requires the permission of International Bible Society. UK trademark number 1448790. Scripture quotations marked ESV are from The Holy Bible, English Standard Version® (ESV®) copyright © 2001 by Crossway, a publishing ministry of Good News Publishers. All rights reserved.

Extracts from The Book of Common Prayer, the rights in which are vested in the Crown, are reproduced by permission of the Crown's patentee, Cambridge University Press.

Excerpts on page 57 from *Murder in the Cathedral* by T. S. Eliot, copyright 1935 by Harcourt, Inc. and renewed 1963 by T. S. Eliot, reprinted by permission of Houghton Mifflin Harcourt Publishing Company.

Published in conjunction with MacGregor Literary.

The text paper used in this book has been made from wood independently certified as having come from sustainable forests.

British Library Cataloguing Data
A catalogue record for this book is available from the British Library.

Printed and bound in Great Britain by Clays Ltd, St Ives plc.

Contents

Prologue

In the movie *Nacho Libre*, Jack Black plays Nacho, a preposterous worker in a Mexican orphanage who has a secret life as an incompetent professional wrestler. There is a scene where he and his scrawny wrestling partner assess their competition – two vicious-looking men in the opposite corner. It appears to Nacho that his life as a wrestler will end immediately in serious injury. In a horrible Spanish accent, he says to his partner, "Pray to the Lord for strength." His partner immediately replies, in only a slightly better accent, "I don't believe in God. I believe in science."

While that bit of dialogue appears in a comedy, it is a statement that is echoed in serious conversations throughout the world. Conventional wisdom seems to say that one either believes in God, or one believes in science. There is no third option.

We, the authors of this book, don't believe this at all – and neither does the subject of this book, physicist and theologian John Polkinghorne. We hope you won't either, when you have finished reading it!

Much has been written about faith and science; the history of supposedly major conflicts and minor harmonies between the two; the rational and irrational accounts from people who read just one of the two books set before us – the Bible we all know and love and the Book of Nature, God's astonishing creation; the condemnation and condescension of one group toward the other. There is a lot of diatribe, but not much dialogue.

We illuminate this issue by writing about John

Polkinghorne – probably the most significant voice in this generation's conversation about science and religion. What we offer is not a conventional *biography* of him. We didn't read his correspondence, interview his family members, students and colleagues, or search databases for public and private records. Instead, we tell the *story* of Polkinghorne, and along the way, we also unfold some bigger issues. How do we know what "Truth" is? How does a leading scientist think about the more mysterious aspects of faith – prayer, miracles, life after death, resurrection? How should people of faith approach science, especially when new scientific discoveries appear to contradict their religious beliefs? It is in telling the story of John Polkinghorne that we manage to grapple with these questions.

Between 2007 and 2010, we conducted many interviews with Polkinghorne. Wherever the book shows a quote from him without an endnote, it came from a personal interview. These interviews occurred in the following locations: Quincy, Massachusetts; a monastery in Venice, Italy; the President's Lodge at Queens' College (while the president was away) in Cambridge, England; the chapels at Trinity College, Queens' College, Trinity Hall and Westcott Seminary – all in Cambridge; the parlor of Queens' College; the Senior Combination Room at Queens' College – under both his own portrait and that of the queen; the study and the sitting room in his home in Cambridge; walking from the vicarage to his old parish church in Blean, England; in his car to and from Blean; at the Good Shepherd Church in Cambridge; and in pubs throughout Cambridge.

As if to cosmically underscore the need for this book, when we approached passport control at London's Heathrow Airport for a final series of interviews with Polkinghorne, the officer there asked why we were coming to England.

"For a conference at Oxford," we said.

"What's the conference about?" he asked.

"God and physics," we replied.

"God and physics, eh?" He paused and looked at us. "Which side are you on?"

Exactly.

CHAPTER ONE

Intellectual Suicide

Events at the Smithsonian's Museum of Natural History in Washington DC are generally tame affairs – lectures for grown-up eggheads who never could understand why their classmates ran so eagerly out the door when the middle school bell rang. On 16 April 1999, however, the eggheads were riled as they took sides in a debate between two seasoned intellectuals. Some worried that the event might even deteriorate into a brawl – if not between the debaters on the stage, then among the agitated crowd in the audience. *The New York Times* would later compare the evening to Jerry Springer's television show.

The electric nature of the debate didn't come from politics, and the combatants were far from being politicians. Nor was the topic climate change, gay marriage, drugs, race, sex, or any of the countless other topics that animates the endless conversations of Washington DC. The combatants charging up the room were physicists, their heads recently pulled from mathematical clouds to engage the topic of cosmic questions: "Why Are We Here?"; "Was There A Beginning?"; "Is the Universe Designed?"; "Are We Alone?". Strong feelings orbit tightly about these questions, and one Georgetown University student in the audience said, "I was almost waiting for it to deteriorate into a physical fight."[1]

The fact that two elderly mathematical physicists could generate this much heat speaks to the rising profile of this field over the past fifty years. In the early part of the twentieth century, "scientist" often meant "chemist," and these scientists were generally pictured as uncontroversial and uninteresting fellows in lab coats, working to develop new medicines, longer-lasting paints, or even exciting new compounds like plastic. But all this changed in 1945 when the first atomic bomb was exploded in the desert of New Mexico, not far from the secret mountaintop facility where it had been created by a new breed of scientists. These new scientists didn't wear lab coats and were notorious for their inability to function in the normal world. These scientists were *physicists* – whatever that meant – and they possessed extraordinary powers to pull terrifying genies out of Mother Nature's bottles.

After World War II, sociologists would turn their attention to this new community of "theoretical physicists," hoping to shed light on this strange new kind of scientist. These scientists were not the subdued chemists of yesteryear who fitted so naturally into the business mold and were comfortable working nine to five in a necktie and short-sleeve shirt. The theoretical physics community, especially in America, was a peculiar and unprecedented *meritocracy*. Identifying the leader on a group project was almost impossible; they all dressed the same, in outfits similar to those worn by the janitor but less color coordinated. First names and nicknames were common and deference seemed to go with raw intellectual prowess, and not with titles or degrees. The physicists worked irregular hours, wore the same rumpled clothing for days, and were untroubled by dishevelment and general chaos. The great platonic world in which they lived was located entirely inside their heads, and things were very orderly there. Studies would later reveal that the average IQ of these physicists was 170.

Within a few years little boys – and eventually little girls – who were good at math dreamed of becoming physicists. It was as close to becoming an authentic magician as the world offered. Physicists transformed our understanding of reality. The atom was a multilayered onion of mystery with strange things the physicists whimsically called "quarks" at the center, held in place by "gluons". The universe was expanding and had begun in a Big Bang, these magicians explained. Exploding stars, black holes, alternative universes, time travel, and other exotica moved out of science fiction and onto the pages of their journals. Equations and diagrams suggested to an uncomprehending public that physicists were indeed uncovering something both real and transcendent. They were drilling into the mind of God.

Theoretical physicists became the oracles of a generation convinced that the deepest truths arise from pages filled with mathematical scribbles and not from the pronouncements of gurus or the interpreters of sacred texts.

And so it seemed strangely appropriate that the Smithsonian's Museum of Natural History, in the very room where the two great astronomers Harlow Shapley and Heber Curtis debated in 1920 one of the great questions of their time (the size of the universe), would invite two theoretical *physicists* to do battle on the great questions of *our* time.

In one corner of the ring was Steven Weinberg, a Nobel Prize-winning physicist with an intimidating presence and a strange, deep voice that seemed to speak for reality itself and not merely the sober fellow possessing it. Weinberg had imposing credentials. He had studied at Cornell in New York, the Niels Bohr Institute in Copenhagen, and Princeton University, New Jersey. He did post-doctoral work at Columbia, Harvard, Berkeley, and Massachusetts Institute of Technology. He had been poached from Harvard by the University of Texas at Austin for an ungodly salary that only an institution built on oil money in a state with an inferiority complex could imagine paying.

Weinberg's research focused on what physicists call "strong interactions" – the forces deep within atoms that keep the positively charged protons from repelling each other and exploding out like popcorn. Weinberg's work has contributed to what scientists know about radioactivity, gravity, medical treatments, electromagnetism, and energy. His theories have illuminated the origin and evolution of the universe. His book, with the remarkable title *The First Three Minutes* described the development of the universe immediately after the Big Bang, and became a classic of science exposition, establishing Weinberg as a brilliant thinker who could explain complex issues to a general audience.

In contrast to the elegant formulations in his head, Weinberg's experiences in the so-called real world had been messy and disturbing. His Jewish parents immigrated to the United States in the early 1930s, settled in New York City, and lived under the dark cloud of anti-Semitism. His mother's family remained in Germany and many of his relatives died in the Holocaust. His encounter with the evils of this world, coupled with the austerity of the theories that describe the development of the universe, have convinced Weinberg that one must not look for a purpose in the world.

In the other corner of the ring and, in some sense, the universe, was John Polkinghorne, a British physicist whose clipped accent, genial manner, and elfish demeanor stood in stark contrast to that of Weinberg. Polkinghorne's deeply mathematical work helped us to understand that the world is ultimately made of those peculiar particles named quarks – the building blocks on which all physical reality is constructed.

Unlike Weinberg's tortured path through the twentieth century, Polkinghorne's journey was a comfortable stroll. He grew up in a religious family, where he came to believe that the world was ordered by a loving creator and filled a rich purpose that flowed steadily into his own life. By the time he appeared at the Museum of Natural History he had completed a distinguished career in physics at the University of Cambridge, been to seminary, become an ordained Anglican priest, and written more than twenty books on the subject of theology.

Polkinghorne's work on quark theory earned him countless recognitions. He was inducted into Britain's Royal Society, an organization dating back to the 1600s when the country's scientific intellectuals began gathering to talk about the new science. Isaac Newton was one of the Society's early presidents. Polkinghorne is one of only two clergy who are members of the Royal Society. He is also the former president of Queens' College, Cambridge, one of the world's most prestigious institutions, begun in the mid-1400s.

Polkinghorne's writings and lectures brought a deeply scientific approach to the exploration of faith, developing new and sometimes controversial approaches to theology. He became an important international figure, an elite thinker taking a scientist's approach to the Bible and its evolving doctrine, as well as to the workings of the universe. His writings and lectures till the troubled soil where science and theology intersect.

Polkinghorne embodies the argument that a thinking person can also be a person of faith, the best example of which is his book *The Faith of a Physicist*, based on the lectures he gave in the internationally acclaimed Gifford Lecture Series. In 1997, he was knighted by Queen Elizabeth II for distinguished service to science, religion, learning, and medical ethics – a rare occurrence since intellectuals are rarely knighted; and in 2002 he was awarded the Templeton Prize, one of the world's largest cash honours, for his contributions to religion.

The showdown at the Museum of Natural History was a clash of two titans of science – similarly trained theoretical physicists who, one might think, would hold identical views of the world. How could a world described by mathematical equations be otherwise? But despite their similar education, titles, and prestige, they live in two worlds. Weinberg believed that the intellectual pursuit of science supported his atheism, revealing, as he wrote so eloquently at the end of *The First Three*

Minutes, "the more the world seems comprehensible, the more it also seems pointless."² Polkinghorne believed that science supported belief in a loving, creative God who people could know personally. How could these two similar geniuses look out on the same world and yet see such different realities?

Polkinghorne knew he could hold his own in a debate against Weinberg. What he wanted to communicate was that religion doesn't tell science what to think, but religion makes science *intelligible*. Religion gives insight. The physical world of science is where the laws of nature hold, but the physical world is only *part* of ultimate reality. In the spiritual world is a deeper reality. "I knew that I knew about these things," he said, reflecting on the event. "I wasn't trying to score debating points. I just wanted to be honest. I wanted to be a Christian witness that we don't have all the answers."

Polkinghorne also knew he need not fear his opponent for, despite Weinberg's atheism and Polkinghorne's Christian faith, the two were actually friends. Polkinghorne had even confided in Weinberg in his kitchen in Cambridge when he was about to leave the university for seminary. Weinberg expressed respect for Polkinghorne's decision, although he would later write that, when Polkinghorne broke the news to him, "I almost fell off my chair."³

Weinberg, for all his bombast about science demolishing religion, is surprisingly spiritual in private and even in his popular writings. "Every time I am with Steve privately, he wants to talk about God," Polkinghorne says. "But he also has a public persona and that night he was very dismissive of me. I heard that he even read a newspaper during my remarks."

Weinberg is known for his scorn for people of faith. "With or without religion," he wrote, "good people can behave well and bad people can do evil; but for good people to do evil – that takes religion."⁴

For years Weinberg has publicly criticized scientists like

Polkinghorne who have a Christian faith. Faith, Weinberg believes, has no place in the world of science, or any other world for that matter, and most scientists he knew didn't think enough about religion to even bother calling themselves atheists.

Aware that the debate about to begin could erupt into rhetorical flames, Polkinghorne found a quiet place backstage to pray. Like the traditional Anglican he has been for his entire life, he recited the prayer he often prays before events like these, taken from the Anglican *Book of Common Prayer*:

> *O God, because without you we are not able to*
> *please you,*
> *mercifully grant that your Holy Spirit may in all*
> *things direct and rule our hearts,*
> *through Jesus Christ our Lord, who lives and reigns*
> *with you and the Holy Spirit, one God, now*
> *and forever. Amen.*

After stating their opposing beliefs and putting up with the surprisingly rowdy audience, the debate ended amicably, with the scientists seated next to one another at a table, fielding questions. Weinberg said that proof of the existence of God could occur right then and there.

"Suddenly in this auditorium a flaming sword may come and strike me for my impiety," said Weinberg, tongue firmly lodged in cheek, "and then we will know the answer." Polkinghorne leaned toward him and disagreed, "Actually, we won't, but that's by the way."[5]

A few minutes later Weinberg returned to the flaming sword image. "The religious mystery is, well, a mystery of whether any of it is true... because unless the flaming sword descends, unless miracles start happening again in a reproducible way that they haven't, there will never be any way of being certain about religion."

Polkinghorne responded "May I just say that, God forbid,

if a flaming sword were to come and decapitate Steve before our very eyes, that would pose a very big theological problem."

Weinberg's rejoinder could have been prepared by Woody Allen: "Well, it would pose not only a theological problem, but a janitorial problem."[6] The audience laughed, as did the combatants.

The prayer Polkinghorne prayed before the debate was the one he had said twenty years earlier in 1979, as he prepared for a much smaller audience in his office at Cambridge, the first time he spoke openly about his conflicting vocational commitments to physics and the priesthood. The academic year was ending, and it was time to select two post-doctoral students from outside the university to continue their research.

Polkinghorne's office was on the first floor of a hundred-year-old building that used to house the university's printing press. The building was tired, its stone façade crumbling. There was nothing quaint or delightfully British about the three-story structure; it was packed into its surroundings like so many of the university's facilities. The interior was equally bland, with the exception of the contents of one cupboard in a lecture hall. The cupboard held a blackboard with equations preserved for eternity by a clear coat of varnish. The equations had been written years before by a visiting lecturer named Albert Einstein.

The building had spacious rooms, including a tea room large enough to accommodate faculty and graduate students from the research areas housed in the building: particle physics, general relativity and cosmology, astrophysics, fluid mechanics, and solid mechanics. Reflecting their natural territoriality, though, scientists from each of these areas sat at different tables in the tea room.

Polkinghorne's office was large enough for the five colleagues to gather and choose the post-doctoral students to continue at Cambridge. The faculty gathered in his office knew each other well. Two were former students of Polkinghorne's. They discussed eight candidates, evaluating their strengths and weaknesses, and reached an easy consensus within twenty minutes. After a few moments of silence, the professors gathered their papers and began shuffling their feet, indicating they were ready to be dismissed.

"Before you go," Polkinghorne said, "I have something to tell you."

The tiny audience settled back into their chairs.

"I am leaving the university to enter the priesthood. I will be enrolling in seminary next year."

There was stunned silence in the room for several seconds. Peter Landshoff, a long-time colleague, broke the silence: "I did not foresee this, but had I been told that you were going to leave physics, I would have guessed what you would do next." Another colleague said, "I don't know what to say, but I am moved by what you've told us." One atheist in the audience was both wistful and wary: "You don't know what you're doing."

Polkinghorne's announcement of his impending transformation from physicist to priest was big news in that small community, and it didn't take long for word to spread. Even in the tea room, the tables that normally held separate conversations, converged on a common question: "John, what were you thinking?" They worried he was committing intellectual suicide.

The question on everyone's mind was not just about a great physicist and his decision to leave academia for the parish. In addition to it being a question about their colleague, which it certainly was, for Polkinghorne was a beloved and respected member of their small community, it was also a larger question about the relationship between faith and science. This question had been discussed in universities, churches, and communities for centuries, long before Darwin put it on the front of papers and into American courtrooms.

"What is the relationship between faith and science?" had been on the front burner all through the nineteenth century in England. Those asking the question often struggled to reconfigure religious belief to accommodate threatening new ideas from both biblical scholarship and new scientific discoveries about origins. In the last decades of the twentieth century, as Polkinghorne was about to take a quantum leap from physics into the priesthood, the question had evolved into something dismissive and pedestrian: Why would an intelligent person have any faith at all?

For Polkinghorne, the question that came from around the world was not "Why do you want to be an ordained priest?" They were deeper questions, and more specific: Why are you a Christian believer in the first place? How can anyone as smart as you believe in such incredible things? Surely differential equations and virgin births can't exist in the same head. Weren't such quaint religious commitments long gone from the scientific community, especially from the elite members of the Royal Society? Hadn't science established that religious belief was archaic, obsolete, intellectually corrosive, and certainly incompatible with the scientific temperament?

The wariness of Polkinghorne's colleagues is time-honored, and easy to understand, especially on the hallowed ground that runs from the University of Cambridge to its ancient rival, the University of Oxford. Once bastions of religious orthodoxy, these venerable institutions used to be controlled by the Church of England and their faculty forced to swear allegiance to Anglican doctrine. Even the great Isaac Newton was once fearful of losing his job at Cambridge for his heretical interpretation of the Trinity. The religious patronage and sponsorship that was so instrumental in launching these great institutions eventually became something of a straitjacket, as scientific advances began to intrude on traditional religious beliefs.

In the nineteenth century these tensions led to a

simmering resentment of the political power of the church, and emboldened leaders began to work aggressively to undermine its influence. As science grew in prestige, it became politically expedient to suggest that religion retarded scientific advance, and polemicists began to sift through history for material to create an argument that religion has always opposed the advance of knowledge. Despite this contrived and artificial reasoning, religion gradually came to be seen as superstitious and hostile to learning and open inquiry. Copernicus and Galileo, both loyal Catholics, were transformed into victims for the cause of science. Galileo became the poster boy for the incompatibility of science and religion, despite his own eloquent insistence that there was no such incompatibility.

With appropriate creativity, polemicists discovered that every scientific advance could be spun into a conflict between science and religion. All that was required was to locate some religious leader who railed against the new science and present the person as representative of the religious response in general.

In the late eighteenth and early nineteenth centuries, science provided explanations for natural phenomena previously ascribed to God's creation and activity, explanations that, although typically developed by Christians, were used by anti-religious zealots to argue that science was slowly destroying religion. Lightning rods in church bell towers, to use one practical example, protected the buildings from what had previously been interpreted as outbursts of God's wrath. When bolts of electricity no longer caused the structures to crumble, it showed, as John Hedley Brooke has noted, that "An ounce of scientific knowledge could be more effective in controlling the forces of nature than any amount of supplication."[7]

Another more dreadful but similar example was the plague, which terrorized Europe and Asia from the fourteenth to nineteenth centuries, wiped out thirty percent of the population in China and killed 35 million Europeans in two years on one of its rampages. The destructive power of the disease made it apocalyptic to religious leaders, who viewed it as the end of the world as described in the book of Revelation and explained it as an act of God, not science. Ultimately, the humble and ubiquitous rat was found to be the culprit, not God or Satan, and generous distributions of poison ended the epidemic.

Such cases often had strong minority voices opposing the scientific explanations but, more typically, the scientists were themselves religious and were simply discovering new things about the world that did not trouble them as believers. But the view that science and religion are incompatible because of religion's irrational insistence on the enduring truth of its ancient texts had taken hold. This view exerted enormous influence on cultural perceptions of religion and religious intellectuals like Polkinghorne in the twentieth century.

Empowered by this myth, voices emerged that challenged the need for religious faith at all, and the twentieth century was the first to have a sizable share of intellectuals who were enthusiastic atheists, from Bertrand Russell and Jean Paul Sartre to Isaac Asimov and Richard Dawkins. The twenty-first century has witnessed the emergence of the so-called "New Atheists," who are like the old atheists on steroids. Not content simply to argue that there is no reason to believe in God, they argue that it is actually *harmful* to believe in God. In fact, religion is *the* problem of the modern world, according to the more prominent New Atheist voices – Christopher Hitchens, Sam Harris, Jerry Coyne, Daniel Dennett, and the omnipresent Dawkins.

These critics of religion have different perspectives, but similar themes: religion and its writings are produced by flawed people; the sacred texts were written too long after the actual events they describe to be trustworthy; people have done horrible things in the name of religion; children should not be indoctrinated by their parents. If you are a person with a religious faith, you must be naïve, ignorant and simpleminded, by the lights of the New Atheists. Hitchens writes in *God is Not Great: How Religion Poisons Everything*, that religion cannot help one's search for ultimate truth. "If one must have faith in order to believe something... then the likelihood of that something having any truth or value is considerably diminished."[8]

Harris, in *The End of Faith: Religion, Terror and the Future of Reason*, and *Letter to a Christian Nation,* focuses on the problem of evil: If God created everything, then God created evil, too. If not, why didn't he stop evil from occurring before it happened?

The last member of this unholy trinity is Dawkins, the brilliant Oxford zoologist and, like Polkinghorne, a Fellow of the Royal Society. He is widely viewed as one of the world's leading thinkers, and *Prospect* magazine ranked him the leading public intellectual in the English-speaking world. More recently famous for his best-selling book *The God Delusion*, Dawkins has led the charge against religion for decades. His book *The Selfish Gene*, first published in 1976 just three years before Polkinghorne left physics for the priesthood, laments the tendency for human beings to believe in God and to put blind trust into indefensible beliefs. The book argues that organisms live and behave as if they have dreams and goals, but they really don't. The apparent purposefulness is just a trick played on them by their genes.

Other Dawkins writings continue that theme. In a subtitle under a chapter of his book *River Out of Eden*, that was published in *Scientific American*, the editors wrote, "Humans have always wondered about the meaning of life. According to the author, life has no higher purpose than to perpetuate the survival of DNA."[9]

Religion, Dawkins argues elsewhere, using scientific metaphors to great effect, is a harmful virus of the mind. People with faith, he infers, are people with infected minds: "In

'Viruses of the Mind' [an essay from his book *A Devil's Chaplain*] I developed this theme of religions as mind parasites, and also the analogy with computer viruses... To describe religions as mind viruses is sometimes interpreted as contemptuous or even hostile. It is both."[10]

The trouble with religion and thinking people, Dawkins asserted on Bill Maher's television program in October 2010, is that smart people know too much about science to believe in stuff like talking snakes. And people of faith by definition, he and Maher agreed, based on their vast and careful surveys of religious people, believe in talking snakes. Elsewhere Dawkins writes that faith is completely alien to evidence or reason, and scientists devote all of their practice to experiments based on evidence and reason. Faith, by these rapidly dimming lights, apparently celebrates lack of evidence as a virtue. And mystery is not only an acceptable "explanation" for what we don't know, but is also a good thing. After all, who doesn't love a good mystery? Scientific ideas, according to Dawkins and most other scientists, are testable, have evidence to support or refute, have precision, are repeatable, universal, and independent of variables such as culture. But "Faith spreads despite a total lack of every single one of these virtues," he wrote.[11]

In this view, intelligent people simply cannot be people of faith because religion is nothing but prejudice passed on to children like a virus being spread maliciously. Science is the domain of truth and evidence. And, as a "lover of truth," Dawkins says, "I am suspicious of strongly held beliefs that are unsupported by evidence: fairies, unicorns, werewolves."[12]

Outside of science, the quest for ultimate truth is foolish, according to Dawkins. Drawing on the myth of perpetual conflict, he argues that faith and science are opposed in every way. The fact that there are so many different religions, many of which contradict each other, proves that God is a delusion.

The 11 September terrorist attacks in New York and

Washington DC in 2001 fueled Dawkins's view that religious belief was not only delusional, but *dangerous*: "Only the willfully blind could fail to implicate the divisive force of religion in most, if not all, of the violent enmities in the world today," he wrote in *A Devil's Chaplain*. "Those of us who have for years politely concealed our contempt for the dangerous collective delusion of religion need to stand up and speak out. Things are different after 11 September. All is changed, changed utterly."[13]

When asked why he is so hostile to organized religion, Dawkins said that he wasn't so fond of disorganized religion, either. "I think a case can be made that *faith* is one of the world's great evils, comparable to the smallpox virus but harder to eradicate," he wrote.[14]

If the purpose of science is to discover deeper realities, then religion does the exact opposite, said Dawkins: "My objection to supernatural beliefs is precisely that they miserably fail to do justice to the sublime grandeur of the real world," he wrote in *The Ancestor's Tale*. "They represent a narrowing-down from reality, an impoverishment of what the real world has to offer."[15]

Dawkins is certainly the most influential scientific soldier assaulting religion, but he has allies. For decades, many high-profile scientists have publicly proclaimed that modern science shatters religious beliefs, making them irrelevant at best, and stupid or dangerous at worst. Common themes in these writings are that religious belief replaces the need for argument, reason, and evidence, and often leads its followers to commit vicious acts. Many prominent scientists conclude that there is no ultimate meaning to the universe and human experience, and that there is no transcendent power outside of what we can measure. Karl Giberson and Donald Yerxa, authors of *Species of Origins: America's Search for a Creation Story*, call this group the Council of Despair, noting that a startling and disproportionate number of the most public voices for science share Dawkins's aversion to religion in any of its forms.[16]

Peter Atkins, a chemist and colleague of Dawkins at the University of Oxford, addressed the origins of the universe in his book *The Creation*, saying that his aim was to "argue that the universe can come into existence without intervention, and that there is no *need* [his emphasis] to invoke the idea of Supreme Being in one of its numerous manifestations." He asks his readers to join him in concluding that there is "nothing that cannot be understood... there is nothing that cannot be explained... everything is extraordinarily simple."[17]

Any leanings that human beings might feel specially created by God in his image are set aside by Atkins. We have "no need to regard ourselves as anything other than the ramifications of chance," he wrote. "This is really the end of our journey. We have been back to the time before time, and have tracked the infinitely lazy creator to his lair (he is, of course, not there)."[18]

Stephen Hawking, the greatest celebrity scientist of this generation, sees science replacing religion. In his biography is this scene: Hawking is in his famous wheelchair, attended to by his nurse, at a restaurant in Cambridge. Twelve students gather around him at the table. Actress Shirley MacLaine joins the group and talks with him for two hours about spirituality and metaphysics. After this lengthy build up she asks him her burning question – whether he believes there is a God who created the universe and continues to guide his creation. Without hesitation, Hawking says "No," in his computer-generated voice. The voice delights his admiring entourage.[19]

In another interview, when asked if God was even necessary, he said, "All that my work has shown is that you don't have to say that the way the universe began was the personal whim of God. But you still have the question: Why does the universe bother to exist? If you like, you can define God to be the answer to that question."[20]

Carl Sagan, who became a media star through his book

and television show *Cosmos*, described the origin of religion as a reaction in primitive cultures to inexplicable aspects of the natural world. Selectively gathering historical episodes that matched his thesis, Sagan said that primitive religions described capricious gods who ran the universe. But the ancient Greeks developed scientific thinking, and their explanations replaced cultures' need for filling in the unknowns by saying "God did it."

He wrote:

> *Suddenly, people believed that everything was made*
> *of atoms, that human beings and other animals had*
> *evolved from simpler forms, that diseases were not*
> *caused by demons or the gods, that the Earth was*
> *only a planet going around a sun which was very*
> *far away. This revolution made cosmos out of chaos.*
> *Here, in the sixth century BC, a new idea developed*
> *– one of the great ideas of the human species.*
> *It was argued that the universe was knowable.*
> *Why? Because it was ordered. Because there are*
> *regularities in nature which permitted secrets to be*
> *uncovered. Nature was not entirely unpredictable.*
> *There were rules that even she had to obey. This*
> *ordered and admirable character of the universe was*
> *called cosmos. And it was set in stark contradiction*
> *to the idea of chaos. This was the first conflict of*
> *which we know between science and mysticism,*
> *between nature and the gods.*[21]

In his 1996 book, *The Demon-Haunted World*, published the year he died, Sagan offers that standard village atheist objection to prayer: "Does prayer work at all? Which ones?... Why is the prayer needed? Didn't God know of the drought? Was he unaware that it threatened the bishop's parishioners? What is implied here about the limitations of a supposedly omnipotent and omniscient deity?... Is God more likely to intervene when many pray for mercy or justice than when only a few do?"[22]

At a memorial service for Sagan in St John the Divine Cathedral in Manhattan, the Revd Joan Campbell said, "He would say to me with a smile, 'You're so smart. Why do you believe in God?' And I would say to him, 'You're so smart. Why don't you believe in God?'"[23]

"Religions are tough," Sagan wrote. "Either they make no contentions which are subject to disproof or they quickly redesign doctrine after disproof. The fact that religions can be so shamelessly dishonest, so contemptuous of the intelligence of their adherents, and still flourish does not speak very well for the tough-mindedness of the believers."[24]

Another leading scientist, Edward O. Wilson, an entomologist who won two Pulitzer Prizes for his books on ants, was raised in a family of Christian believers – Southern Baptists, in fact. But when he began studying biology at the University of Alabama, and then continued at Harvard, he felt released from his religious background.

"I found it a wonderful feeling not just to taste the unification metaphysics but also to be released from the confinement of fundamentalist religion," he wrote. "More pious than the average teenager, I read the Bible cover to cover, twice. But now at college, steroid-driven into moods of adolescent rebellion, I chose to doubt. Most of all, Baptist theology made no provision for *evolution*. The biblical authors had missed the most important revelation of all!"[25]

His study of evolution explained what his religious training could not. Scientific discovery ultimately replaces the need for religion. Religion holds a place for good literature, poetry and sentiment. But only science can provide an objective framework for truth, he contends.

"Religion is also empowered mightily by its principal ally, tribalism," Wilson wrote. "If the religious mythos did not exist in a culture, it would be quickly invented."[26] But passion, sentiment, and fear aren't science – those are the domain of religion, in Wilson's view.

In *Consilience* he wrote:

> *If history and science have taught us anything, it*
> *is that passion and desire are not the same as truth.*
> *The human mind evolved to believe in the gods.*
> *It did not evolve to believe in biology. Acceptance*
> *of the supernatural conveyed a great advantage*
> *throughout prehistory, when the brain was evolving.*
> *Thus it is in sharp contrast to biology, which was*
> *developed as a product of the modern age and*
> *is not underwritten by genetic algorithms. The*
> *uncomfortable truth is that the two beliefs are not*
> *factually compatible. As a result those who hunger*
> *for both intellectual and religious truth will never*
> *acquire both in full measure.*[27]

In *On Human Nature*, Wilson further develops the idea of science's advantage over religion.

> *I consider the scientific ethos superior to religion:*
> *its repeated triumphs in explaining and controlling*
> *the physical world; its self-correcting nature open*
> *to all competent to devise and conduct the tests; its*
> *readiness to examine all subjects sacred and profane;*
> *and now the possibility of explaining traditional*
> *religion by the mechanistic models of evolutionary*
> *biology. The last achievement will be crucial. If*
> *religion, including the dogmatic secular ideologies,*
> *can be systematically analyzed and explained as a*
> *product of the brain's evolution, its power as an*
> *external source of morality will be gone forever.*[28]

Even scientists not on overtly anti-religious campaigns, like the late Stephen Jay Gould, rarely find room within the scientific temperament for genuinely religious beliefs. Gould defines religion until it is unrecognizable in an effort to remove conflict with science. In his book *Rocks of Ages* he writes, "Science tries to document the factual character of the natural world, and to develop theories that coordinate and explain these facts. Religion, on the other hand, operates in the equally important, but utterly different, realm of human purposes, meanings, and values – subjects that the factual domain of science might illuminate, but can never resolve."[29]

And this, of course, brings us back to the debate at the Museum of Natural History, with the views of Steven Weinberg, Polkinghorne's friend and sparring partner. In *The First Three Minutes* Weinberg defined his views on the relationship between religion and science with these memorable lines:

> *It is almost irresistible for humans to believe that*
> *we have some special relation to the universe,*
> *that human life is not just a more-or-less farcical*
> *outcome of a chain of accidents reaching back to*
> *the first three minutes, but we are somehow built*
> *from the beginning… It is very hard to realize that*
> *this all is just a tiny part of an overwhelmingly*
> *hostile universe. It is even harder to realize that this*
> *present universe had evolved from an unspeakably*
> *unfamiliar early condition, and faces a future*
> *extinction of endless cold or intolerable heat.*[30]

Then came his famous sentence, quoted above, about the more comprehensible the world is, the more pointless it is.

Still, something calls us to think beyond ourselves, even if there is no real point to it, he writes. He concludes the book with what became a widely debated statement on our search for truth and meaning.

> *But if there is no solace in the fruits of our research,*
> *there is at least some consolation in the research*
> *itself. Men and women are not content to comfort*
> *themselves with tales of gods and giants, or to*
> *confine their thoughts to the daily affairs of life; they*
> *also build telescopes and satellites and accelerators,*
> *and sit at their desks for endless hours working out*
> *the meaning of the data they gather. The effort to*
> *understand the universe is one of the very few things*
> *that lifts human life a little above the level of farce,*
> *and give it some of the grace of tragedy.*[31]

Years later he reflected on that last statement and wrote, "I ended [the book] with a description of our world as a stage, onto which we have stumbled with no script to follow," he wrote. "But the tragedy is not in the script; the tragedy is that there is no script."[32] In his book *Dreams of a Final Theory*, he takes on the notion of the existence of God directly.

One chapter begins with a psalm of David: "The heavens declare the glory of God; and the firmament showeth his handiwork." But since the time of the psalmist, Weinberg asserted, there isn't any wonder about stars any more – science told us what they were. "The stars tell us nothing more or less about the glory of God than do the stones on the ground around us," he said.[33] There is no mystery left. What had been ascribed to the handiwork of God has all been explained. As the laws of nature are discovered and understood, believing in God becomes unnecessary. "All our experience throughout the history of science has tended toward a chilling impersonality in the laws of nature," he wrote. Evolution, is the final dagger into the heart of religion. "Judging from this historical experience, I would guess that, though we shall find beauty in the final laws of nature, we will find no special status for life or intelligence... And so we will find no hint of any God who cares about such things."[34]

Weinberg gets personal in *Facing Up*: "My life has been remarkably happy, perhaps in the upper 99.99 percentile of human happiness, but even so, I have seen a mother die painfully of cancer, a father's personality destroyed by Alzheimer's disease, and scores of second and third cousins murdered in the Holocaust. Signs of a benevolent designer are pretty well hidden. The prevalence of evil and misery has always bothered those who believe in a benevolent and omnipotent God."[35]

In his debate with Polkinghorne, Weinberg emphasized the need to get past what he considers religion's false assumptions. If religion searches for meaning and moral order, he said, it might as well give up – there is no meaning and moral order. "My passion about this arises from regret that it isn't true," he said, speaking honestly. "But if it isn't true, then surely it's better that we not kid ourselves into thinking that it is. It's better that we salvage what we can from at least the satisfaction of creating some meaning around us."[36]

He was even more direct in other writings, where he said he hoped science would once and for all "eliminate the wishful thinking, mysticism, and superstition that pervades much of human thought, even among physicists."[37] Weinberg thinks we should all grow up. "If that's the way the world is, it's better we find out. I see it as a part of the growing up of our species, just like the child finding out there is no tooth fairy. It's better to find out there is no tooth fairy, even though a world with tooth fairies in it is somehow more delightful."[38]

Ultimately, science has given smart people a reason to not be religious, he said. "One of the great achievements of science has been, if not to make it impossible for intelligent people to be religious, then at least to make it possible for them not to be religious," he wrote. "We should not retreat from this accomplishment."[39]

At a conference at the Salk Institute in La Jolla, California, Weinberg described religion as a crazy old aunt: "She tells lies, and she stirs up all sorts of mischief and she's getting on, and she may not have that much life left in her, but she was beautiful once. When she's gone, we may miss her."

Dawkins, at the same conference, wasn't so sentimental about the crazy old aunt. "I won't miss her at all," he said. "Not a scrap. Not a smidgen."[40]

And yet, in the middle of all the anti-religious saber rattling, there is Polkinghorne, neither rattled nor defensive about being a person of faith. A priest, even. Polkinghorne did not take a combative stance against Weinberg in the debate, but searched instead for common ground. Looking at Weinberg he said, "I think the fundamental difference between you and me is this: We both want to take human persons seriously but we take them seriously in radically different ways. You see human persons as constructing a world of meaning which is a sort of oasis of meaning in a vast desert of a hostile and meaningless universe."

Weinberg nodded. "I see us not constructing meaning… but I see us *discovering* meaning," Polkinghorne said. "In fact the world has a meaning that extends beyond us. That's the basic difference between us."[41]

Polkinghorne acknowledges that science doesn't have all the answers. He played an important role in the work that determined that the quark is the smallest particle. It was a major scientific discovery, and a widely heralded one. But what doesn't get mentioned is that no one has actually seen a quark. Scientists have confidence that quarks exist because believing in their existence explains other things. Other scientific knowledge makes sense if it includes the belief that quarks exist.

Even Weinberg conceded this at the debate."We don't believe in quarks because we've seen them," he said. "We believe in quarks because the theories that have quarks in them work."[42]

This, of course, was exactly Polkinghorne's point. Scientists of faith do the same thing with spiritual realities that scientists – with or without religious faith – do with their beliefs in physical realities. The quarks and gluons, and a host of other explanatory elements in science, are accepted as real because they do so much to help make sense of the world. Religious claims, of course, are not testable and objective in the same way as scientific claims, but this is a matter of degree, not kind. The assertions of the New Atheists that science is completely objective, and religion is completely subjective are simplistic caricatures that betray a profound confusion about the limits of both science and religion.

In both his science and his faith commitments, Polkinghorne embraces Michael Polanyi's thinking, taken from his influential book, *Personal Knowledge*. Polkinghorne summarizes Polanyi's thinking into this maxim: "To commit myself to what I believe to be true, knowing that it may be false." Polanyi, a Hungarian philosopher and chemist in the first half of the 1900s, rejected the idea that scientists were purely objective. Scientists were not heretics, as some were claiming at the time, but were part of a *community* trying to establish beliefs and dogmas, he argued. The scientific community, therefore, was not that different from the religious community. All knowledge is personal, said Polanyi, and observers cannot separate themselves from their backgrounds, experiences and judgments.[43]

Weinberg's experience of being raised in a Jewish home and having members of his family die in the Holocaust will, by definition, have an impact on the interpretations he makes in his scientific pursuits, according to Polanyi. Likewise, Polkinghorne's experience of being raised in an Anglican home and his brush with death as an adult will also have an impact on the interpretations he makes in his scientific pursuits, *even if the scientific pursuits are the same*. Science gets its great strength from its ability to rise above these limitations and build an objective picture of the world. But it would be a mistake to suppose that science does this perfectly, or to suppose that religion cannot do it at all. "All human knowing involves perception from a particular point of view, which will offer opportunities for insight but be bounded by its inherent limitations," Polkinghorne said.

Both science and faith are means by which we seek to understand ultimate realities. But they are different in how they look at those realities and what questions they ask. Polkinghorne likes the homey and quintessentially British example of making a pot of tea: A person observes a kettle of water on a stove and asks, "Why is the water in the kettle boiling?"

One answer – the sort provided by a scientist – is that burning gas is creating heat, which raises the temperature of the water to the boiling point. Another answer is that the kettle is boiling on the stove because I am making tea – and would you care to have a cup with me? Both responses are valid and in touch with reality, Polkinghorne says, and they certainly don't need to cancel one another or even compete. In fact, the two explanations complement each other, providing a more complete picture of the tea-making enterprise, answering more questions, and giving the activity a rich and satisfying description. The two explanations are "friends, not foes" he says.

In *One World*, Polkinghorne wrote, "Theology and science differ greatly in the nature of the subject of their concern. Yet each is attempting to understand aspects of the way the world is... They are not chalk and cheese, irrational assertion compared with reasonable investigation, as the caricature account would have it."[44]

Nor are they identical. There are many ways to see religious principles in everyday life, Polkinghorne believes. "Our goal is an integrated picture of the way the world is," he continued in *One World*. "In that picture science and theology, reason and revelation, all find their place. There is indeed revelation of God, in those particular events and understandings preserved in Scripture and tradition, but it is not insulated from the critique of reason or from evaluation in association with other forms of insight."[45]

Some of the difference between faith and science lies in the motivation for seeking truth. "Religious motivations are more akin to the sort of motivations that lead us to trust our friends; that is they are attained through trusting rather than testing," he said.

As for the atheists who say these different pursuits of truth cannot travel the same road, Polkinghorne is undaunted. He doesn't accept their characterization of religion. Many of his colleagues are, to be sure, wary of religion. But that is because they believe that people with faith must believe in what their religious authorities tell them to believe.

"Religious belief isn't shutting your eyes, gritting your teeth, believing six impossible things before breakfast because the Bible tells you that's what you must do," he said at the debate with Weinberg. "It is a search for a *motivated* belief – a difficult search and different people will reach different conclusions about it. But you don't have to commit intellectual suicide to be a religious believer; otherwise I wouldn't be one."[46]

How Polkinghorne's faith came to create such a shift in his vocation, leading him from the laboratory into the parish, goes back to one of Christianity's most ancient traditions. It is a sacrament that draws scorn and ridicule from many scientists, and it is at the heart of Christian belief: the Mystery of the Eucharist.

CHAPTER TWO

Room for Reality

World War II witnessed countless messages. Some precipitated great movements of troops and hardware; some contributed to long-range strategy; some were created to deceive. Cryptographers on both sides worked feverishly to code and decode the communications going back and forth. The majority of the messages of this war were small communications however – often a simple letter or telegram letting a family know that one of their loved ones was missing in action, or else had been killed.

Peter Polkinghorne, John's older brother, fought in the Royal Air Force. The RAF served so heroically fighting the Nazis that an emotional Winston Churchill was moved to immortalize their effort with these famous words: "Never in the field of human conflict was so much owed by so many to so few." Peter Polkinghorne's fighter plane, like so many others, went missing somewhere in the North Atlantic. Shortly afterwards, the Polkinghorne family received one of those tragic messages that had been sent to so many other families. Their response, so common in homes all over the world during World War II, was to pray.

John was twelve at the time the message about his brother arrived in 1942. He prayed to God that Peter would be found. Maybe the squadron had just been blown off course, the family reasoned. The weather *had* been terrible, after all. And Peter was an expert pilot. Surely he would have figured out a way to survive and eventually return to his family, armed with tales of great adventure. God would surely save Peter. Look at all the people praying for him!

The hope that the squadron would be found lasted two days. Peter and John's father came home early from work, his face the color of a warship's hull. It was clear that Peter and the others in his plane were at the bottom of the Atlantic. John burst into tears. His mother, an active member of the local Anglican parish, felt that God had let her down. She resented God's failure to prevent Peter's death. When the parish vicar came to the house to pray with her, she refused. Reflecting on this nearly sixty years later, Polkinghorne adds, wryly, "But she also didn't like that vicar."

Peter was just twenty-one when he died. Before the war, he had been impressed by the academic potential he saw in his little brother, even calling John "professor" in his letters. "I was, of course, greatly saddened at the time of his death," John recalls, "but recovered in the way that twelve-year-old boys do, not because they are heartless but because they live so much in the unfolding present."[1] Today, almost seven decades later, Polkinghorne continues to live in the unfolding present.

Street, the town where the Polkinghorne family lived during the war, was in Somerset, near the port city and manufacturing center of Bristol, a popular target for German bombing runs. John and his parents would be awakened at night by air raid sirens, and then lie awake listening to the German planes fly overhead, drop their bombs, and then return to Germany. Sometimes the family hid under their staircase. Later at night they could see the glow of Bristol on fire. Occasionally the planes even went overhead during the day.

John was eight when the war began. "I didn't have a realistic view of the war as a child," he said. "I saw it as a drama – a scary reality that I was carried away with."

Peter was the second child that the Polkinghorne family had lost. Before John was born, his sister Ann had died at six months from an intestinal blockage. Because of complications during her pregnancy, doctors recommended against John's mother having any more children. "She was bold enough to ignore their advice," he said.[2] It was difficult for his mother to be with other families that had more than one child. No photos of Ann were on display in the house, but John's father routinely visited her grave to keep it tidy. The only time John's mother saw his father cry was when Ann died – he didn't even cry at the death of his own mother.

Although John's mother felt abandoned by God when her two children died, she remained a devout Christian. She was gifted with a welcoming and hospitable spirit to the degree that total strangers would sometimes trust her with their life secrets. She and John's father, a Post Office employee, took John to church every week. "I cannot recall a time when I was not in some real way a member of the worshipping and believing community of the Church," he recalls, looking back. "I absorbed Christianity through the pores, so to speak, perhaps to a greater degree than a more direct form of instruction would have conveyed." John enjoyed church, and liked the vicar (the one his mother didn't), who, in John's eyes, had the ability to bring Bible scenes to life.

John also liked school, especially math, where, like so many prodigies, he showed an early aptitude. His mother instilled in him a love for literature, especially Charles Dickens. He did not fare so well with music. Full of self-confidence because of his other school successes, Polkinghorne remembers taking a music test at the neighborhood Quaker school, anticipating he would again receive the top grade in the class. Most of his answers, however, turned out to be wrong. He was humiliated at this ignominious introduction to his personal limitations.

As with Dickens, he developed an appreciation for Shakespeare, literature, and some poems. But the world's true poetry, he slowly discovered, was more clearly displayed in an elegant mathematical equation than in a well-crafted verse.

"There is a thrill in encountering a beautiful equation which I believe is a genuine, if rather specialized, form of aesthetic experience," he said, echoing a sentiment that mathematicians have shared since Pythagoras first began to celebrate the glories of numbers twenty-five centuries earlier.[3] Polkinghorne loved the clarity of the specific, the elegant symmetry and "rightness" of mathematics, in contrast to the vague symbolism of poetry.

Grief over Peter's death had some unspoken, if not inevitable consequences for John. He was the only child left of three, and a pressure to achieve took hold, as if he had inherited an obligation to contribute to the world on behalf of his deceased siblings. He obsessed over being the best student in his classes, and came to expect his name to be always at the top of every list. Once, he missed several days of elementary school because of bronchitis, which resulted in some of his grades being unavailable for a critical grading period. When the rankings came out, there were three names ahead of his on the roster, which he found most disturbing.

Regardless of the subject, young John dutifully checked his homework over and over before handing it in. Once, as he was turning in a math test, he realized he had misunderstood the directions, and got the entire test wrong. When he explained this to the headmaster, the "daunting man" replied, "If *you* got the directions wrong, then what chance does the rest of the class have?"

Polkinghorne's achievements as a youth got the attention of the headmaster of the grammar school, who decided to meet with Polkinghorne's father. The headmaster said that John would be better served at a school with other high-achieving students, and recommended that the Polkinghornes send their rising mathematical star to the Perse School in Cambridge, where he would be academically stretched. "My parents valued the intellect," he said. "It got you on in the world. Going to private school meant I was part of an elite group of scholars, which meant a lot to my mother." It also meant taking a thirty-minute train to Cambridge from Ely (where the family now lived), then a twenty-minute walk from the train station to the school, and then the return trip. The commute kept John from being very active in school events, but he did perform occasionally with the school's theatre group, play rugby, and edit the school magazine.

The Perse School buzzed with high achievers working toward getting their School Certificates with distinction. "I thought of myself as unremarkable, except for academic achievement," he said. "I didn't need any outside pressure to motivate me."

It was here that the young John's love for mathematics – he called it "an entrancing subject" – took off. Like generations of mathematicians before him he found that what was opaque and incomprehensible one week was clear and obvious by the next. This led to increasingly complicated thinking as he solved ever more complex equations. His capabilities measurably increased by the week and he acquired a growing sense of what mathematicians refer to as their "power". This trajectory could take him only to university, and most science-minded achievers at that time looked toward Cambridge rather than its rival, Oxford. John's teachers and headmaster advised him to apply to Trinity, one of the colleges in the University of Cambridge, where the most famous of all mathematicians, Isaac Newton, had studied and then taught 300 years before.

Trinity College had a system where each student was appointed his or her own don, or tutor, who advised and looked after the student. It was the ultimate mentoring arrangement, and the don was much more than an academic advisor, looking out for the overall welfare of the student to whom he was assigned. Part of the lore about the don assigned to Polkinghorne included the way he proposed to his wife, which sounded like a line from a script about science geeks: "Jane,

Jane, how would you like to see my name on your tombstone?" This romantically challenged don persuaded Polkinghorne to apply for a major scholarship at Trinity and not even bother applying to other colleges such as King's, Queens', or any of the other prestigious locations in the Cambridge system. It was a risky move, but the don knew a star when he saw one, and Trinity awarded Polkinghorne a major scholarship.

Before he could begin at Trinity, however, he and most of his contemporaries had to fulfill their military obligations. He set aside his slide rule and math handbooks and spent a few months marching, assembling and disassembling his rifle, and plunging his bayonet into faux-Nazis made of straw. The recent war made the training rigorous and serious, but it was actually the inspections in the barracks that made him most anxious. "One officer struck the fear of God in me by declaring my bunk area a 'pig's breakfast'. That was very nerve-wracking."

Polkinghorne's military service gave him his first teaching experience. As an eighteen-year-old he was assigned to teach elementary mathematics to technical apprentices preparing to become electrical and mechanical engineers. He enjoyed the experience immensely, discovering that teaching fitted his personality. His love for teaching kept growing after his military service when he entered Trinity College, and made his home in hallowed precincts still haunted by the ghost of Isaac Newton.

Trinity has an ancient feel to it. Its origins go back to the 1300s, and it was in 1546, three years after Copernicus published his revolutionary book on the motion of the earth, that King Henry VIII combined two schools to create Trinity. The college beckons students into its courtyard through a gate that includes a sculpture of its founder in the archway. The interior grounds include an immaculate and immense rectangular lawn, with living quarters, classrooms, a library, and a chapel taking up the perimeter. Isaac Newton once lectured in one of those classrooms – but there was no one there to hear his words; his contract specified only that he deliver lectures, not that anyone attend them. There is even a tree that, legend has it, was grafted from the grove of apple trees Newton observed when they were dropping their apples and inspiring his thoughts about gravity.

The library at Trinity was built by Sir Christopher Wren, and it holds a rare eighth-century copy of the letters of St Paul. In addition to Newton, Trinity's long list of celebrated undergraduates include Francis Bacon, John Dryden, George Herbert, Alfred Lord Tennyson, Lord Byron, Bertrand Russell, Ludwig Wittgenstein, Jawaharlal Nehru (India's first prime minister), A. A. Milne, Alfred North Whitehead, and Vladimir Nabokov. The college has produced thirty-two Nobel Prize winners.

Polkinghorne's training in this superstar atmosphere included being given mathematical problems to solve on the spot. The problems appeared simple at first, but were in reality quite complex and the goal was not merely to solve them, but to solve them *immediately*. Examinations at Cambridge required that students do original thinking to solve problems they had not seen before. It was like a debate, only with numbers. One of his dons – a Russian – would present Polkinghorne problems to solve on a crumpled piece of paper. No matter how quickly Polkinghorne solved the problem, the professor would say things like, "I am surprised that so good a mathematician as yourself would not be able to do this problem." It was the perfect kind of motivation for an emerging mathematical prodigy who had been competing with himself since elementary school.

The exalted world of mathematics beckoned. Its rich patterns were like sirens, seducing anyone who could hear their song. Those patterns and the remarkable processes they empowered opened up a broader understanding of the physical world. That broader world drew him in deeper with every equation.

But the doors to broader world vistas opened by mathematics were not the only things beckoning Polkinghorne at Trinity. On his first Sunday as a student, he attended Holy Trinity Church with a group of other students who were part of the Christian Union. During the service, the preacher recounted the story of Jesus' encounter with Zacchaeus, a reviled tax collector. In order to see Jesus, the diminutive Zacchaeus had to climb a tree. Jesus called out to Zacchaeus, the two met, and the tax collector's life was transformed forever. Jesus, the vicar told the congregation, was on his way to Jerusalem where he would be crucified, so this was the only time he would pass that way. Had Zacchaeus not acted on that opportunity when he did, who knows what his life would have become? The vicar then told the students they had the opportunity that day to have their lives transformed in the way Zacchaeus' life had been changed. This was their opportunity, he told them, to offer themselves to Christ and to be made new. When he invited those who desired this transformation to come to the front of the church, a group of students responded, including Polkinghorne: "I felt a call for a change and moved to the front of the church."[4] While not the sort of "devil to saint" conversion that can be turned into a novel and a roadshow, Polkinghorne sensed that it was a deepening, or intensifying experience that built on what had begun in his home.

"It was more of an epiphany moment than a conversion," he said. In the army he had regularly attended chapel services, but he felt that his lifestyle was not wholly consistent with a follower of Christ. In this service at Holy Trinity he believed he had a moment of commitment – "a course correction," he called it. The hymn they would sing before communion was "Let All Mortal Flesh Keep Silence". Verse one reads:

> *Let all mortal flesh keep silence,*
> *and with fear and trembling stand;*

ponder nothing earthly-minded,
for with blessing in his hand,
Christ our God to earth descendeth,
our full homage to demand.

And while the experience led him to study Scripture rigorously, pray, and attend worship services regularly, an atmosphere of rigidity enveloped the Christian faith, as it was lived out by John and his fellow members of the Christian Union. Instead of a liberating experience, it seemed legalistic, narrow-minded, guilt-inducing, fearful of other points of view (including other Christian traditions), and inhibiting. "There was a certain bleakness that seemed to be expected of the faithful, which cast something of a shadow," he said.

Years later he sensed liberation from those shackles, through the disciplines of the Anglican Church. An emphasis on daily prayer and Scripture reading, as well as on the mysterious sacrament of the Eucharist, gave him a freedom that filled him with a lifelong joy.

But in an age where science seems to increasingly answer many of life's big questions, one can justifiably ask why would Polkinghorne – or anyone else, for that matter – believe in God at all?

For Polkinghorne, part of the answer derived from a dynamic tension in his scientific work. The more he committed himself intellectually to science, the more he came to appreciate that science was often not as objective as it appeared to be. One of the great cultural myths about science, as noted in our introduction to this book, is that it deals only in facts, and that the beliefs of the scientist are irrelevant to the experiments that are the basis for these facts. John came to appreciate that the quest for truth in science emerges from a context and that context always had a deeply subjective character, rooted in the scientist's motivations. The belief that science has facts and religion has opinions mischaracterizes both science and religion.[5] Instead, they are intellectual cousins.

Polkinghorne's view resonated with Michael Polanyi's articulation of this point. In *Personal Knowledge* Polanyi integrated scientific understanding with the person pursuing the understanding. "Complete objectivity as usually attributed to the exact sciences is a delusion and is in fact a false ideal," he wrote early in the book.[6] In Polanyi Polkinghorne saw more clearly that we all have reasons for what we believe and what we don't believe. The reasons may come from upbringing, education, evidence, experience, or instinct, which Polkinghorne likes to call "motivated belief". People of science are *motivated* to believe certain things as they proceed with their experiments. People of faith are *motivated* to believe certain things about God as they proceed with their beliefs.

The more he read Polanyi, the more he connected with the message. "I had already read a lot about the philosophy of science," Polkinghorne said, "But when I read Polanyi I thought, 'This chap knows what it's like to be a scientist.' He was a player in the game. I would read it and say, 'Yes, that's right.' There was an authenticity to it." Armchair philosophers of science, who try to understand it "second-hand" by looking in the window, so to speak, often describe science in ways that practicing scientists find unfamiliar.

Our beliefs can both steer us toward truth, or away from truth, even if we're trained scientists, Polanyi said. "During the eighteenth century the French Academy of Science stubbornly denied the evidence for the fall of meteorites, which seemed massively obvious to everybody else," Polanyi wrote. "Their opposition to the superstitious beliefs which a popular tradition attached to such heavenly intervention blinded them to the facts in question."[7] The claims of Copernicus, Kepler, and Galileo, that the earth orbits around the sun instead of the popular vice versa version maintained by the more traditional thinkers, were based on facts and mathematical arguments available to all astronomers at the time. But the beliefs of each scientist motivated some to interpret the observations one way, and others to interpret them another.

As Polkinghorne had experienced earlier in his career, with mathematical insights opening up into bigger and more complex equations and knowledge leading to an unfolding of the patterns of the universe, he resonated with Polanyi's description of creative scientists: "We call their work creative because it changes the world as we see it, by deepening our understanding of it. The change is irrevocable. A problem that I have once solved can no longer puzzle me; I cannot guess what I already know. Having made a discovery, I shall never see the world again as before. My eyes have become different; I have made myself into a person seeing and thinking differently. I have crossed a gap, the heuristic gap which lies between problem and discovery."[8]

But it was Polanyi's lack of certainty – even in his work as a scientist – that drew Polkinghorne to his overall approach. Noting that both Kepler and Einstein were correct in *some* of their assessments, and incorrect in others, but that both were led by their impulses and passions, he said, "They were competent to follow these impulses, even though they risked being misled by them." As for himself as a scientist, Polanyi said, "What I accept of their work as true today, I accept personally, guided by passions and beliefs similar to theirs, holding in my turn that my impulses are valid, universally, *even though I must admit the possibility that they may be mistaken*."[9] (Emphasis added.)

In other words, after all their training and education, after all the experimenting and validating of their findings, scientists step out as human beings and propose what they think is true. But they might be wrong.

Science, by these lights, is a set of *beliefs* which scientists are motivated to accept, not a set of *truths* that can't be called into question by those motivated to be skeptical about them. Doubting is as important to science today as it was to the Greek philosophers in the fifth century BC.[10]

That kind of humility in science seemed as rare to Polkinghorne in his college years as it does today. But it is consistent with his approach to both science and faith. Polanyi said, "I must aim at discovering what I truly believe in and at formulating the convictions which I find myself holding." Discovery, Polanyi said, "is guided by personal vision and sustained by personal conviction."[11]

Columbus, to take a famous example, was mostly wrong about reaching the Indies. He correctly followed the maps of previous explorers, but the maps happened to be inaccurate. But he was right in believing it was possible to reach one part of the world from the other. "He had committed himself to a belief which we now recognize as a small distorted fragment of the truth, but which impelled him to make a move in the right direction. Such wide uncertainties of its aims are attached to every great scientific enquiry."[12] Polkinghorne would hasten to add that those uncertainties are attached to faith pursuits as well.

"I liked that he talked about being open to correction," Polkinghorne said. "His lack of certainty was a great relief." But that lack of certainty was not what Polkinghorne was hearing from his fellow students in the Christian Union. "They thought that their certainty was reality, but they were mistaken. What was so good about Polanyi was his belief that it is rational to commit yourself to what you believe to be true, but it needs humility and caution. It's the same thing in human relationships. No marriage is ideal, for instance. People have a fantasy ideal for what marriage is, like it's a succession of à la carte choices. "It was a great relief to read that you didn't have to sign up for everything – that there was room for maneuvering – room for reality," he said.

Remarkably, even though religious uncertainty was present and even affirmed in Polkinghorne's faith quest, somehow he avoided going through an atheist phase. He's not sure why, other than to say that he was more motivated to believe than to not believe. His friend and fellow scientist/theologian Alister McGrath was an atheist who became a believer, but "I have never been outside the worshipping and believing community," he said.

Still, Polkinghorne believes atheism has a point. "There's an argument for it," he said. Atheism, however, has simply not attracted him, despite what some of his fellow scientists have experienced. "I am puzzled by Richard Dawkins," he said. "He's giving science a bad name. Christianity doesn't have a clean slate, but to skate over Pol Pot, Stalin and Hitler is dishonest. His book *The God Delusion* is full of assertions, not argument, and it's incredibly naïve. It's like saying the earth is flat because I can't see the bend in the earth from my window. I wish he'd just shut up."

The assertion that science is fact and religion is opinion makes a double mistake, in Polkinghorne's view. "Facts always come with interpretation," he said. "Science is easier, because it has a greater degree of agreement because of experiment. I have never thought that the atheist scientists might be right. Even as a young person I thought it was unfortunate that they don't believe."

Recalling Polanyi, Polkinghorne said, "I have motivations for my believing in a creative God." Such a belief cannot be proven but it can be motivated. "It's a reasonable position, but not a knock-down argument. But it's strong enough to bet my life on it. Just as Polanyi bet his life on his belief, knowing that it might not be true, I give my life to it, but I'm not certain. I'm as certain as I am in judging people's character. Sometimes I'm wrong."

He did not join or remain in a believing community

because of a supernatural event, either. "I am a rather humdrum Christian, more drawn to the sacraments than to the spectacular," he said. "During worship I don't get claps of thunder, but there's an authenticity that I experience in worship, and I am grateful." He has a stronger "negative faith" than he does a "positive faith". He occasionally wavers and continues to wonder. But there's something liberating about not needing to know for sure. "When you pray through the psalms, which I do, you see a lot of wavering and wondering," he said. "The psalmist has no qualms about expressing doubt. *Intellectually* I am unwavering when it comes to committing myself. *Spiritually* I'm not. Some people are given the gift of untroubled faith. It is not my gift."

At times he ponders whether the Christian faith is too good to be true. "When I question like that, I say to myself, 'Then dismiss it and turn away from it.' But I can't. It's not because it's all serenity, either, because it's not. It's more like Psalm 13, where we lament, yet we trust in God. People who have periods of doubt have a deeper commitment." And while he has never "gone to the depths of disbelief," he has had plenty of doubts. "I quiver with the notion that I may be mistaken. But I choose to stand with Christ."

His concept of God emerged in those days of listening to Bible stories in church as a child; God was an unseen friend in whom he could trust; but now God is something beyond human thinking. "It's still developing. I became more aware of my limitations and finiteness of my imagination, in a similar way as when I moved from an understanding of classical physics to quantum physics. God is unseen and will never totally be known by finite beings."

Polkinghorne's concept of God now includes descriptions such as a "Divine Mind", and "Cosmic Mathematician", but who also cares for the individual. That care for the individual is shaped by the life, death, and resurrection of Jesus Christ. "The cross is deeply mysterious – sacrificial death and resurrection. That enriches my view of God," he said, comfortably affirming the central and most challenging part of Christianity.

Just as he would do as a scientist, he looks at religious faith from a variety of angles to see if the answers make reasonable sense. There are a lot of important things that can't be proved, he says. Can a person *prove* that another person is really his friend, and not just being agreeable out of self-interest? Or can one *prove* that it's wrong to rob a blind man?[13]

Polkinghorne is drawn by *unseen* forces to the Christian life. Not because of what science reveals to him, or what his rational mind tells him. He is drawn to it in part because of what happens during a worship service. "Most of my heightened experience with the divine comes during worship – the Eucharist and Wesley hymns especially. The hymn 'Thine Be the Glory' still brings tears to my eyes." Verses two and three of that hymn are:

> *Lo! Jesus meets us, risen from the tomb;*
> *Lovingly He greets us, scatters fear and gloom;*
> *Let the church with gladness, hymns of triumph*
>   *sing;*
> *For her Lord now liveth, death hath lost its sting.*

> *No more we doubt Thee, glorious Prince of life;*
> *Life is naught without Thee; aid us in our strife;*
> *Make us more than conqu'rors, through Thy*
>   *deathless love:*
> *Bring us safe through Jordan to Thy home above.*

Science and faith have some common ground, he believes: "Science *involves* an act of faith. We are taught skills and end up knowing more than we can tell." Both involve a quest for truth, but they approach that quest by asking different questions. Science can tell us that the world began with the Big Bang, and can beautifully describe the billions of years of aftermath, of an ever-expanding universe in constant tension with the gravitational pull that keeps it all from blowing apart. Scientists really can explain it, in beautiful, elegant mathematical equations. Science tells us how. But it can't tell us why. That's a different question and a different quest.

Francis Collins, head of the human genome project, said in his book *The Language of God*, that science is the only reliable way to understand the natural world, and through science we can gain profound insights into material existence. "But science is powerless to answer questions such as 'Why did the universe come into being?' 'What is the meaning of human existence?' 'What happens after we die?' One of the strongest motivations of humankind is to seek answers to profound questions, and we need to bring all the power of both the scientific and spiritual perspectives to bear on understanding what is both seen and unseen."[14]

"How" or "why" questions do not start from nowhere. They both take interpretation. "You can't just stare at the world," Polkinghorne said. "You have to view it from a chosen point of view." He continued, "Choosing the point of view involves an act of intellectual daring in betting that things might be this way. This means that in science, experiment and theory, fact and interpretation, are always mixed up with each other."[15]

And while science is on a quest for knowing truth, it can't tell us the *whole* truth, because it doesn't ask all of the questions. Religious faith, in its quest for truth, doesn't ask all of the questions, either, but it asks different questions. Science doesn't negate the validity of faith, nor does faith negate the validity of science. They seek truth from different points of view.

But what is religious faith? Faith leaps into the light, not the dark, he says. "The aim of the religious quest, like that of the scientific quest, is to seek motivated belief about what is the case." Religion, like science, can only be of value if it's true.

Both have, at their core, a desire to understand.

"Science is only one slice of reality," Polkinghorne said. "The rest of the world is much more complex. Human affection, ethics, beauty – the limitations of science can't deny the validity of those experiences."

Consider light. For years scientists showed convincingly, with both observations and theory, that light was a series of particles. Later, scientists showed, again with both observations and theory, that it was waves. Scientists then proved that, depending on the situation, light acts like particles some of the time and waves some of the time, but never both at the same time. "In 1899 no one thought that wave/particle duality was possible. That was a rational belief. But if there is motivating evidence, you have to enlarge your view of rationality. There is no universal rationality." But Polkinghorne cautions that the wave/particle duality of light is not a perfect analogy to faith. "The real lesson is that reality is surprising and teaches us not to think we know. Reality should lead us to ask, 'What makes you think this is the case?'"

Sometimes we understand truth better through science, and sometimes we understand it better through faith. As Annie Dillard said in *Teaching a Stone to Talk*, "What is the difference between a cathedral and a physics lab? Are they not both saying: 'Hello?'"[16]

The quest for God, Polkinghorne says, will always be accompanied by a veiled understanding. "It's the only way finite creatures can have free will," he said. "What we are experiencing now is veiled soul-making." But both science and faith include a heavy dose of wonder.

"When you make discoveries, even little ones, they have the qualities of elegance, economy, and fertility regarding their order. The greatest complexities of the world come out of simple equations that could fit on the back of an envelope," he said.

After finishing his undergraduate work at Trinity, in 1954 Polkinghorne received a prestigious fellowship to study processes involving particles much smaller than atoms. The study of the tiniest bits of matter is called elementary particle physics, the field in which he would earn his PhD.

While at Trinity, Polkinghorne was introduced to Ruth Martin, a statistics major at Girton College, by a mutual friend, and the two of them began seeing each other at Bible studies and after lectures. During a vacation they went to a madrigal concert on the bank of the River Cam, with King's College in the background. The trees arching over the river made it an unusually romantic setting, and things between them grew appropriately more serious. "My introduction to her was a great gift, because at Cambridge at that time, there were ten men for every one woman," Polkinghorne recalled with evident pleasure. "I wasn't meeting anyone!" Later they attended the Festival of Britain, a celebration of national pride, creativity and discovery, and they gradually concluded that they wanted to marry each other. Without John's ever saying, "Ruth, Ruth, how would you like to see my name on your tombstone?" they graduated, married, and in 1955 moved to Pasadena, California, where John had a post-doctoral fellowship at California Institute of Technology, or Caltech.

Soon after they arrived in the US, Polkinghorne was watching television and saw four men in tuxedos singing "Give me that old time religion, that's good enough for me." He realized at that point that "The Christian scene in the States was going to have a somewhat different tone from that which we were used to back home."[17] The scene became symbolic in his mind because he thought it illustrated how different American Christianity was to the Anglican Christianity he experienced growing up. "It didn't strike me as goofy, but shall we say it didn't present all the richness of Christ, either."

In his professional research, Polkinghorne was part of the

team that began to challenge the longstanding conclusion that the smallest known particles that made up atoms were protons and neutrons. Experimental evidence suggested that there was something "inside" protons and neutrons. But what could that be? It became clear that those particles were made up of other particles, but no one could see what those smaller particles were. The physicists knew that the particles were "there" but they moved too quickly to be independently observed. Still, because of their experiments the researchers were motivated to believe that the particles inside the protons and neutrons were real. Eventually they were labeled quarks and gluons.

In high-powered accelerators, underlying patterns of activity could be inferred from the observation of collisions. Particles would be smashed into each other at great speed and the resulting "debris" analyzed to see what was going on. The process was very complex and might be compared to trying to understand how automobiles are constructed by smashing them into each other and looking at the pieces that result.

The researchers discovered that the patterns observed in the collisions in the accelerators could be described with mathematical equations. The unknown particles they were investigating had properties in common. In fact, similar components hiding inside protons and neutrons manifested themselves with suggestive regularity but the particles never appeared on their own. It would be like listening to two people talking in the dark but suspecting that it might be a ventriloquist with a dummy. How do you figure out what is going on?

The initial research was high on theory and light on observation. The mathematical arguments seemed compelling but it wasn't clear exactly what the mathematics was describing. A question naturally arose: "Were there any *actual* elements, or was it all just math?" asked Murray Gell-Mann, who won the Nobel Prize in Physics in 1969 for "discovering" the quark. Gell-Mann, paradoxically was not sure the quarks were physically real in any simple sense, and described them as "presumably mathematical". Perhaps they had no real existence outside of the equations describing them. Another scientist, James Bjorken, was able to show that light was bouncing off protons and neutrons in a way that suggested there were real, physical particles inside them. The flamboyant physicist and Nobel Laureate Richard Feynman extended Bjorken's idea, adding support to the idea that quarks were more than just mathematical entities.

Polkinghorne's research team helped make the existence of quarks mathematically precise, so that the models could be more effectively compared with the observations. "I didn't discover the quark. My team made mathematically well-formulated models to show patterns if there *were* these things called quarks. The role my team played in quark understanding is that we made them mathematically respectable."

This experience provides insight into why Polkinghorne can believe in both quarks and God, even though he has seen neither. "Physicists are quite prepared to trust in unseen realities, provided that the indirect motivations for the relevant belief are persuasive," he said.[18]

After a year at Caltech and having attended a Presbyterian church nearby, Polkinghorne left the United States for a job as a lecturer at the University of Edinburgh. Two years later, in 1958, he was back "home", teaching physics at the University of Cambridge. Even though his teaching career was just beginning, he discovered that he had a pastoral concern for his students. He experienced great satisfaction in assisting his students through successes and struggles, especially the students he mentored in research. "Research is difficult, and that is a tricky and formative time for students," he said. "You're dealing with people as people, and seeing them every day. I enjoyed telling them things and helping them. The most difficult to help were those who were most confident."

At Cambridge he headed a research group that helped to further establish what is now the widely held view of quark theory. For his contributions to developing this more complete method of seeing the world, he was inducted as a Fellow in the Royal Society in 1974. Becoming a member of the Royal Society revealed something about himself that surprised and disturbed Polkinghorne. Usually humble and self-effacing, Polkinghorne was startled by how much he obsessed over this award. "If you had to put me in some curious scheme by which my election would have been assisted by the murder of my grandmother, I would certainly have declined, but there would have been a perceptible pause for mental struggle before I did so."[19]

Polkinghorne's own soul-making took what looked like a dramatic turn when he left this distinguished physics career to become a vicar. His spiritual leanings were as strong in his mid-career as they were that first day in Holy Trinity Church when he was inspired by the story about Zacchaeus. As for physics, he felt as if he had done his bit for the subject, and that the future of his specialty was best left to younger people. Mathematical physics, like baseball, gets harder with age. He was forty-seven.

Polkinghorne believed he had responded to his spiritual vocation by using his considerable talents for research and teaching but now it was time to step aside. "Somehow one needs mental agility more than accumulated experience, and it becomes progressively harder for an old dog to learn new tricks."[20] "I wasn't disillusioned with physics – I just didn't want to do it the rest of my life," he said.

So Polkinghorne walked away from physics. Weinberg fell off his chair. Other colleagues looked on in disbelief. But Polkinghorne was more than just a physicist and he had made his mark on that ancient science. Walking away was not difficult. But he wasn't walking *away*. He was walking *toward* a new calling, responding to his growing desire to be a minister of word and sacrament, toward a new life that he anticipated would provide "deep satisfaction".[21]

Polkinghorne's conviction that his spiritual side was rotating toward the sun came when he went on a Trinity College retreat where, except during worship, silence was the rule. Talkative and outgoing, heading off into a cloud of silence seemed like putting on a straitjacket. But he went anyway. He discovered something that many contemplative Christians had found over the centuries – that the rawness and intimacy of shared silence was spiritually rich. "I soon learned how positive is the experience of silence, and how genuinely related you become to the others who are sharing that silence with you," he said. "One can really begin to enter into the inner space that silence opens up."[22]

A neighborhood Bible study led by a Jungian psychotherapist challenged Polkinghorne both intellectually and spiritually. Jung's writings resonated with the physicist morphing into a priest, but it was the group leader, Eric Hutchison, who broadened his theological thinking. Hutchison showed how Scripture can be used to *expand* one's understanding rather than to narrow it. Another friend introduced Polkinghorne to the writings of Jürgen Moltmann, a German theologian whose book, *The Crucified God*, would shape Polkinghorne's views on suffering.

Leaving physics for seminary seemed crazy. Most people assumed Polkinghorne must have had some "Damascus Road" experience. Just as the apostle Paul stopped persecuting Christians, so the Cambridge mathematician was about to stop solving equations, they thought. But there wasn't any bright light or handwriting on the wall. It was much lower key than that, Polkinghorne said.[23] He simply prayed about it with his wife Ruth and close friends, and sought counsel where he could. The sun began to rise over a new horizon and things began to seem clear. He had been a lay reader in his church and the experience sat very well with him. He loved the transcendent mystery of the Eucharist and wanted to help others share that experience.

Not surprisingly, he anticipated his decision would build to a "great climax", but he was disappointed. He spoke to the local Anglican diocese, and was simply told to attend a retreat with other prospective members of the priesthood. "Once I said that this was what I believed I wanted to do, I was told I needed to have my vocation tested by the Church," he said. "I was leaving a world where I was well known and had many contacts, to go to a world where no one celebrated my arrival." These prospective priests were not impressed with his degrees, his research, or even his membership in the Royal Society.

Reflecting on this transition in his life, Polkinghorne said, "Any process of significant change will have its ups and downs, and there will be moments in which you wonder exactly what is happening to you and what you have let yourself in for. At such times, it was encouraging to remember that careful thought had been given by others to the wisdom and appropriateness of the move that you were making."[24]

The time-honored process of entering the priesthood has always been understood in terms of a "calling". Prospective priests need a clear sense that this important step is ordained by God, and right for them. A process of discernment thus precedes official approval. As part of this process, each person on the retreat organized by the diocese was called upon to lead an impromptu discussion based on a topic drawn from a basket. Polkinghorne drew a line from T. S. Eliot's play, *Murder in the Cathedral* – "The last temptation is the greatest treason: To do the right deed for the wrong reason." He turned the phrase around – "Would it be better to do the wrong thing for the right reason?" – and discussed motivation.

Once approved by the diocesan leadership, he announced he was leaving academia, giving up mathematical physics for theology. The transition, while certainly dramatic, had one major continuity – both subjects pursued truth about the world. He found that orthodox Christian belief was "both surprising and exciting, in the same way that a good scientific theory enlarges one's imagination and satisfies one's intellectual desire for understanding," he said. "I'm driven by the need to take both science and religion seriously, and I'm sure that they are friends, not foes, in the common quest for knowledge."[25]

Thus it was that in 1979 former mathematical physicist John Polkinghorne, colleague of Paul Dirac and Abdus Salam, professor to Martin Rees and Brian Josephson, Fellow of the Royal Society, and destined to be knighted by the queen, could be seen several times a week on Cambridge's ancient streets riding his bicycle to Westcott House, an Anglican seminary in Cambridge. At Westcott, he worshipped each day in a small, simple chapel, a fraction of the size and spectacle of the one at Trinity. The platform was plain, of the sort one would find in a country church.

Polkinghorne and his seminary classmates read the Daily Office (a combination of Old and New Testament readings, songs generated from the psalms, and prayers of reflection), and recited morning and evening prayers. These ancient disciplines, dating from the early centuries of the church, encouraged a deepening of faith. He especially appreciated the brutal honesty of the psalms, which carried both praise and complaint to God, cries of anger, and vows of trust, demands that God "wake up" and see what was happening, and honest devotion.

Polkinghorne was almost twice the age of most of his classmates; he had already earned a PhD and had been married for more than two decades, as well as having raised three children. Not surprisingly then, he often played a role of older brother to his junior colleagues.

At Westcott, Polkinghorne developed his view that God

must be experienced and understood as *personal* – a God who enters into every aspect of our existence. Moltmann had pressed this point in *The Crucified God*, where the cross of Christ is articulated as the means by which God participates in the suffering of the world. Moltmann's ideas profoundly influenced Polkinghorne and shaped his views on everything from evil and suffering to the doctrine of the Trinity.

Polkinghorne pastored in hospitals as a part of his training – first in a ward with leukemia patients, and then in a ward with people suffering from anorexia. He learned to come alongside, literally, those who were suffering, entering into their predicament. Polkinghorne recalled one woman who could not bring herself to her husband's bedside during his painful experience. The former mathematical physicist gently took her hand, led her to her husband's bedside, and sat with the two of them until the suffering eased. "There was no magic word or magic action that would make everything all right, but there was a modest kind of tacit and respectful alongsideness that could be offered, both through presence and through prayer," he said.[26]

He worked with handicapped children, and learned to love them and their caregivers, who seemed empowered by an infinite patience and love. And no matter how confined or limited the children were, he learned, deeply and profoundly, that "there could not for a moment be a doubt that they were persons, with all the worth and respect that attaches to that."[27]

These pastoral experiences deepened his conviction that religious belief is a reasonable quest for truth. "Some of the people I know who seem to me to be the most clear-eyed and unflinching in their engagement with reality are monks and nuns, people following the religious life of prayerful awareness."[28]

Polkinghorne had taught himself Greek while on a research project in Switzerland, and was voracious in his

New Testament studies. And he loved the practical training – preaching, serving the Eucharist, leading the Daily Office, conducting baptisms. The practical training, unfortunately, did not include music. It was assumed that students brought that ability with them to school, a woefully incorrect assumption in Polkinghorne's case. He had failed his early childhood musical tests and never addressed the problem. As a result he had trouble even figuring out where to start a song he was supposed to lead. At a vespers service for a group of nuns he was handed the music and expected to start the song. But there was no organ to give him an opening pitch, so he had to guess at a starting note, an exercise in applied mathematics. He guessed high. The nuns did their best to follow him but, as the song went higher, they had to screech. The next night he overcompensated and started too low. He now recommends that priests include tuning forks as part of their equipment, in addition to their Bibles and prayer books.

At the heart of Polkinghorne's theology is his unshakeable conviction that God loves and God cares. But, unlike so many glib apologists today, he realizes there is plenty of motivation to *not* believe and that many honest seekers cannot find their way to faith. The presence of evil and suffering in the world – the very concern raised by Weinberg in the famous debate we mentioned in the opening of this book – is one of the chief reasons. "I can see why it holds people back, if they have terrible experiences," he said. "It isn't just the existence of evil and suffering that is problematic – it is the *magnitude* of it. Some experience it and transcend it, others are crushed by it."

He agrees that it doesn't always look like God is at work in the world. "Does a world with cancer and concentration camps really look like the creation of a powerful and loving God?" he asks.[29] Polkinghorne notes at least two dimensions to the question of suffering. One has to do with the choices people have made throughout civilization to inflict great cruelty on others. If one believes in free will – and Polkinghorne does – then men and women must be free to do both good and evil. The possibility of committing evil and immoral acts is the price humans pay for not being puppets. A more vexing problem, though, comes from nature, where people suffer mightily under the oppression of disasters and disease. What about tsunamis that wipe out thousands of innocent people? Nobody's free will caused that.

Polkinghorne's response is consistent. Just as the evil actions of people are a corollary of their free wills, so natural evil results from nature's freedom to continue to follow its own laws as it makes itself. That's why tectonic plates keep shifting, hurricanes keep storming, droughts keep drying. "I do not believe that God directly wills either the act of a murderer or the incidence of a cancer. I believe God allows both to happen in a creation that has been given the gift of being itself."[30] Tectonic plates shift, for example, and bring minerals from deep down to the surface of the earth to replenish crucial resources. But those same shifts are called earthquakes, and often create disasters of the sort that occurred in Haiti in 2010 while this book was being written. "There is an inescapable shadow side to the evolutionary process. It will yield not only great fruitfulness, but there will also necessarily be ragged edges and blind alleys. The engine that has driven the development of life on Earth has been genetic mutation."[31]

The suffering in the world is not the signature of an uncaring, weak, or indifferent God, says Polkinghorne. Suffering flows from a creation that is allowed to "be itself". But while telling a young mother that her cancer is not a divine punishment or a consequence of divine indifference is true, it is not helpful in her circumstances. Neither is it helpful to tell her it is a necessary by-product of the evolution of new life, and Polkinghorne acknowledges this.

The mystery takes him back to Moltmann, where God

is not somewhere "out there" in celestial repose while we're "down here" in the vale of tears. The Christian God, through the crucified Christ, participates in the suffering alongside us. God comes alongside us in the darkness and bitterness and embraces it with us. There is suffering, but we're not alone in it; God was there at Auschwitz when Weinberg's relatives were being led to the gas chambers. "One of my main reasons for being a Christian is that Christianity speaks to the problem of suffering at the deepest possible level," he said. Instead of a spectator God, Christianity involves One who knows suffering from the inside.[32]

It was this suffering God that came alongside Polkinghorne at a crucial point in his parish ministry – as he lay in a hospital bed wondering if he was going to die.

Droplets of Grace

It was 1983, Polkinghorne's doctor was worried. His patient needed emergency care and things didn't look good. With some effort, John's wife Ruth had been located and rushed to his side, perhaps for a final goodbye. Polkinghorne was in a great deal of pain and extremely weak. He knew he might not survive and that the goodbye he said to Ruth might be his last.

"There was no outburst of external emotion," he recalled years later, "but a feeling of committing myself into God's hands." Polkinghorne had been losing strength for weeks and had excruciating abdominal pain. His appetite was gone, and he had lost considerable weight. He took his condition seriously, of course, but not *that* seriously – he was British, after all – and his doctor tried different medications to relieve the pain. Nothing worked. When the pain got worse the doctor discovered that Polkinghorne had a ruptured colon, and was about to die. Emergency surgery was the only option. The last words he heard before the anesthetist put him under were, "You have a wonderful surgeon." It was a comforting thought, Polkinghorne remembers thinking, as he drifted off.

He woke up in the Bristol Royal Infirmary's recovery room (having moved back to Bristol to work as a curate). He was in extreme pain and could barely move. His eyes drifted toward the intravenous fluid dripping from the bag on the pole next to his bed into a tube that fed into his arm. That seemed to be his entire world. A drip would form at the bottom of the bag, then drop into the tube, then trickle toward the needle in his arm. Another drip formed in its place, like a runny nose. He seemed in some alternate universe with only one activity that depended strangely on him. All of his strength was focused on getting each drop of the magical fluid out of the bag, into the tube, and on to his arm. Bag to tube to arm. Bag to tube to arm. For the bag to work properly in this alternate universe, he thought it needed his cooperation and concentration. Any lapse in attention could render the bag dry. His life had become a series of short fragile episodes, nourished one drip at a time. "My world collapsed into the size of that IV bag," he said.

The mental exertion exhausted him. He felt so weak he was sure God had abandoned him. He couldn't pray. For several weeks he was in the hospital. There were weeks of rehabilitation, two additional surgeries, a period with a colostomy bag.

As things began to settle down, he found that he was sustained, not only by the IV bag, but by the knowledge that his family, his church, and some of the Anglican nuns he had befriended were praying for him. He felt that he was being kept alive by the prayers of others, tiny drops of grace working their way from God to his emaciated body. Twice, as he hovered at the border of consciousness, he had visions of one of the sisters kneeling in prayer in a chapel, as he had seen them do many times. "I was learning something of the communion of saints and the power of prayer," he said.[1] Those who were praying for him seemed to be saying, "Don't worry. If you can't reach out to God yourself in your weakness, we'll be your carriers, so to speak, of the communication between God and you."[2] Tiny drops of grace.

Did it really matter that people were praying? To be sure, the prayers were "answered" in the affirmative and Polkinghorne recovered. But many people do not recover and most prayers are not answered in the affirmative. He remembered the prayers on behalf of his brother Peter, whose fighter plane was never found. Prayer, in fact, has yet to pass a scientific test of its effectiveness. A 2006 study by researchers at the Harvard Medical School showed that, not only did patients not improve after major heart surgery while knowing that people were praying for them, many actually were worse off than those who did not have prayers on their behalf.[3] But why would a scientist, especially a *physicist* who understands that the body is a complex molecular machine, believe in prayer in the first place?

Molecules do what they do. They react with one another and cause reactions. They join together; they separate, often in unpredictable ways. That's how the world is. Can prayer change things – make molecules do something different than what they would do on their own? If so, why doesn't it *always* change things when we pray or at least change things in a way that would be statistically discernable?

People had asked Polkinghorne these questions for much of his adult life, usually on the heels of asking him why a scientist would believe in God. Many could accept the belief in God part of faith – after all, the laws of physics are pretty awesome and they don't explain themselves. But prayer? That was like believing in magic.

"But it's not magic," he said. "When we pray we aren't using the occult or other spiritual powers to produce what we want. And it's not a matter of our needling God, or pounding our fists on the door of heaven. We're not telling God something he hadn't noticed."

Prayer is central to religion. It is complex and confusing, despite what a 2009 *New York Times Magazine* article reported. That writer quoted a rabbi who said that prayer comes down to saying four things: "Gimme! Thanks! Oops! and Wow!"[4] Prayer may indeed involve, as the rabbi said, petition, gratitude, forgiveness, and worship. But prayer also involves meditation and reflection, confession, and a desire for unity with the divine.

When Polkinghorne was young he prayed the "Gimme!"

prayer, especially around examination time: "Please God, help me pass this exam." But even at the age of seventy-nine he found himself praying similarly when he lost his garage key one night as he walked from his garage to his house. An irrational fear came over him as he imagined a thief catching a glint of light reflected from the key as it lay in the grass, leading to the thief opening the garage and stealing his car. He prayed in an irrational panic, went outside late at night with a flashlight to search for the key and did not find it. The next morning, after an anxious night, he went back outside and, with the help of bright sunshine, found the key. He prayed that he would find it and he did. The next day. After a rough night.

Most of the time Polkinghorne's prayer life is contemplative, silent, aligning his spirit with God's. Sometimes he takes the Jesus prayer – "Lord Jesus Christ, Son of God, have mercy on me a sinner" – and says it over and over "so it will dissolve from my mind to my heart," he said. Other times he repeats a Scripture. "You need help getting into the silence, and sometimes a mantra helps," he commented. The repeated phrase helps him become aware of his breathing, of his back against the chair, his feet on the floor, his hands open, and provides room for God. One phrase from Scripture is popular at spiritual retreats, but he doesn't like using it. "The phrase 'Not my will but thine' is one I use with certain reluctance," he said. "It gives God a way out and doesn't expect too much of him."

As for praying the Jesus prayer, does Polkinghorne really consider himself such a sinner that he needs to repeat *that* prayer with such frequency? "When that prayer was written in the Orthodox Church, the emphasis was on sin and the cross – it was the fruit of the time, and the balance was skewed," he said. "Today's prayers have a better balance, I think, where they reflect that we all know that we fall short. Few have that intense feeling of Luther, for good or for ill. Sin now is more of an ethical matter."

Polkinghorne uses icons to assist his prayer life. He has a copy of the icon he and his Westcott classmates commissioned, of a majestic Jesus holding a book on which the verse "You did not choose me; I have chosen you" (John 15:16) is written. Sometimes gazing at it helps him reach into his spiritual dimension more deeply. Like a mantra, an icon serves as a focus of attention. It's not supposed to be realistic, like a photograph or a painting. "It's a visual reminder that our contact with God is not just intellectual," he said. There are other levels of knowing and communicating. "It's one thing to say 'hallelujah,' and another thing to sing 'The Hallelujah Chorus'. It's a different focus and a different encounter with reality." He looks at the Westcott icon and considers the words of Jesus. "It's both intellectual and confrontational," he said.

Polkinghorne's pastoral training included visiting people in hospital and, of course, praying for them. But he knew that not everyone who was prayed for would be healed. Then why do it? From a pastoral perspective, prayer is for the sick and dying and, while it may not bring about physical healing, it does bring the suffering into the presence of God. "There was no magic word or magic action that would make everything all right, but there was a modest kind of tacit and respectful alongsideness that could be offered, both through presence and prayer."[5] Sometimes all he could honestly pray for was a peaceful acceptance of one's circumstances. Sometimes there isn't an answer.

"I didn't want to be offensive, but I didn't want to do just anything to be loved," he said. "There may not be a particular reason for a person's condition. That's a very difficult message, but important. Meaning and fulfillment may not be found in this life."

In one wing of the hospital where patients with leukemia were in great pain, Polkinghorne would sit at bedsides and tell patients who he was, whether they appeared conscious or not. He rarely spoke to them about theology. He didn't try to intellectualize their suffering by explaining that evolution is a series of genetic mutations and that those mutations have a dark side that can lead to leukemia. His alongside presence was mostly nonverbal. "I saw my limitations," he said. "I hope my presence brought about an intuition of peace and home. I never thought there would be a miraculous remission of their condition. All any of us can do is be with people and mediate the presence of God."

In one parish he visited a family with a child who was dying of cancer. The family, stricken with an all-too-common grief, asked why God was punishing them. "There is a lot of folk religion out there," he said. "It's better than nothing, but not enough." The thinking of this family, and others like them, was that if they could just get on the right side of God, then the cancer would go away, or that they would win the national lottery, or even that you might find your lost key. "Sometimes you have to make a guess about what questions they can't bring themselves to ask. The most common question is: Why is this happening? It's not because God is angry and is punishing you. It is a mystery we aren't able to penetrate. These things just happen. Sometimes all I can say to some people is that their child is in God's safe keeping."

The mystery of spirituality hovers around the sick and dying. So many questions about the meaning of life, suffering, and death are posed and answered there. Francis Collins, for example, the famous American scientist who led the genome project and went on to head the National Institutes of Health, witnessed religious people in hospitals when he was a young doctor. As a medical student, he visited sick and dying patients and was often struck by their deep spirituality. Usually that manifested itself in an unnatural peace the patients experienced, despite their dire circumstances, despite their suffering, and despite the fact that they had not brought these diseases on themselves. "If faith was a psychological crutch, I concluded, it must be a very powerful one," Collins said. "If it were merely a cultural construct left over from more primitive times, then why weren't these people raging against God instead of talking about him in a loving manner?"

One encounter with a dying patient started Collins thinking. She had shared with him her Christian beliefs, and then asked him what he believed. All he could do was stammer, "I'm not really sure." He realized that he, a scientist, had never looked at the evidence regarding faith in God. He read C. S. Lewis's *Mere Christianity* and eventually became one of America's leading public figures of faith, an American Polkinghorne championing the compatibility of science and religion.

Collins wrestled with prayer in much the same way as Polkinghorne. From a scientific perspective, prayer was a puzzlement. He found himself longing to communicate with God, however, and understood that prayer was the means for that to occur. "Prayer is not, as some seem to suggest, an opportunity to manipulate God into doing what you want Him to. Prayer is instead our way of seeking fellowship with God, learning about Him, and attempting to perceive His perspective on the many issues around us that cause us puzzlement, wonder or distress."[6]

One of the more primal and troubling aspects of prayer, of course, is the request for God's healing. One of Polkinghorne's acquaintances, David Watson, a prominent evangelist known throughout the world, was diagnosed with cancer in the 1980s. This worried Watson, but he had confidence that this would be an opportunity to show the healing power of God. His colleagues and family gathered around him and prayed for his healing. A pastor friend from California told him, "I don't accept this cancer and I believe that God wants to heal you." The pastor then summoned his entire congregation to pray urgently for Watson.[7]

Other religious leaders gathered around Watson and quoted the verses from James 5:14–15 (ESV), "Is any among you sick? Let him call for the elders of the church, and let them pray over him, anointing him with oil in the name of the Lord; and the prayer of faith will save the sick man, and the Lord will raise him up." Watson had done this very thing with others. People from around the world – including Polkinghorne – made their way to Watson. Others called and wrote to tell Watson that God had told them that he would recover fully. It was an enormous spectacle.

The Californian pastor had a large congregation built in part on the practice of healing prayers. He flew to Watson's hospital room, laid hands on his abdomen, quoted Scripture, cursed the cancer and claimed healing. Watson felt a surge of energy. The pastor told him that the tumor might grow for a little while longer, but that the root of it was gone now, "And soon it will begin to die."[8]

Other congregations conducted special "healing Eucharists" for Watson. The BBC did a special program on Watson and healing. He read about the healing power of positive attitudes, about the need to remove stresses from life, about the need for humor, about the need to forgive others, about the need to let go of bitterness and other aspects that might hinder the activity of God, about the need to have strong faith. And then he died, in almost the exact amount of time his doctors told him it would occur.

When Watson was first diagnosed with cancer, he began writing about it, to provide for the world an account of how God miraculously healed him. The book, *Fear No Evil*, takes a turn toward the end, as he and his family realize that he is not going to recover. The book chronicles pain and comfort, sadness and joy, and throughout, an account of the presence of God in even the most dire circumstances.

"His intent was to keep a diary of his healing," Polkinghorne said. "But it became a diary of his death." The book was a model of Christ accepting his destiny – "It was a Gethsemane kind of book," Polkinghorne said. "I prayed for his healing, but not necessarily his physical healing. I prayed more that he would accept his destiny."

A similar experience occurred with one of Polkinghorne's close friends, John A. T. Robinson, dean of Trinity College, Cambridge, and author of the controversial classic book *Honest to God*. Robinson was given six months to live after being diagnosed with pancreatic cancer. Despite frequent prayers for healing, including placing hands on him by elders in his church, Robinson died in the predicted six months.

Robinson's wife told Polkinghorne what she believed were the fruits of this experience. The prominent Robinson experienced much opposition in his community for what some called his liberal views, she said. But his opponents were moved by the way the Robinsons endured this disease and faced death with courage. As a result, many of the conflicts among the opposing groups were resolved. She also said that while the family was told that Robinson would likely die a painful and stressful death, he died peacefully at home. A different kind of healing had occurred, she said. "No doubt, they had been hoping for something different – some physical remission – but they were able to accept God's will in the form of their sad destiny," Polkinghorne said.[9]

So if God doesn't heal a David Watson despite Watson's ministry and powerful friends praying for him, or John Robinson, who also followed biblical mandates of calling others to pray for his healing, why pray at all?

"We pray because the world is open to the future," Polkinghorne said. "We have free will and can act as agents." Prayer, in Polkinghorne's view, is the desire to align the human will with God's will. So it's acceptable to state to God what one wants. "When I have to see a doctor, I pray 'Lord, may it not be

too serious. I want to stay with my family longer.' That's not a
belief in magic or pulling a lever. But I think it's reasonable to
ask that, and I don't expect God will always do what I ask."

As we saw earlier in this chapter, sometimes the prayers
even involve garage keys. "When I lost my garage key I said,
'Lord, I want to find my key.' I was having anxiety about
it. It seems natural to share my anxiety with God, even if it
seems foolish. God's action takes place in the context of your
relationship with him. In the New Testament story of the blind
man named Bartimaeus, he had to tell Jesus what he wanted.
He had to commit himself to it."

Even when pessimistic about the outcome, Polkinghorne
prays anyway. Health scares and car trouble lead him,
instinctively, to pray. It's a natural outgrowth of his relationship
with God. So is complaining. "It is silly to berate God, but the
psalmist berates God for some serious things," he said. "Asking
'Why me?' is a legitimate question. When I was sick, in the
hospital, and wondering what was to become of me, I said to
God, 'But I was only in my parish for one and a half years!'"

And still, despite the possible futility, we pray. For ourselves,
for others, and for the world. We pray alone. We pray with our
families. We pray in our worship services. The act of asking
implies relationship, even when the asking is misguided. A
farmer's prayer for rain conflicts with that of the pastor who
prays for clear weather for the church picnic. Mark Twain's
bitter *War Prayer* shows how praying for victory for "our" side
means death and destruction for the other side. No doubt the
other side is praying for victory as well. In a poignant scene
from the 2005 movie *Kingdom of Heaven*, one warring side
paints crosses on their shields and goes into battle proclaiming
God's favor on their side. But so does the other side.

Although asking God for something might be childish
or even selfish, it is not inappropriate. Polkinghorne prefers
the term "child-like," which is the posture Jesus endorses in

Matthew 18:3. "We believe in a personal God, and that must mean a God who does particular things for particular people in particular circumstances," he said.[10]

Scientists, suggests Polkinghorne, say prayers of adoration without realizing it. " 'Wonder' is an indispensable word in the vocabulary of a scientist," he said. And prayers of adoration, through wonder, are prayers that have been prayed by followers of God from the beginning. It's when the prayers are petitions, or requests, that scientists have trouble.[11]

Science tries to describe a world that is orderly, regular, and somewhat predictable. We can predict the orbits of planets, the passage of constellations overhead, and even the arrival of comets. The newspapers can print accurate forecasts of when the sun will appear in the morning. Weather doesn't just happen. It's part of how hot and cold air masses flow around the surface of the earth. It gets tricky when scientists think about praying for changes that seem to go against that existing order.

"There is a great deal at stake for Christianity (and I believe for Judaism and Islam too) if we can answer 'Yes' to the question, 'Can a scientist pray a petitionary prayer in a way that is positive, without impugning his or her scientific integrity?' " he said.[12]

In the past century the scientific view of the world has changed in some ways that make prayer less troubling for scientists. The worldview that emerged in the wake of Isaac Newton's discovery of gravity and the later discoveries related to electricity and magnetism was *mechanical*. The world was a grand machine, with interlocking parts that fit tightly together, like the cogs and wheels in an old-fashioned clock. Just as one could not imagine opening up the back of a clock and changing something without totally disrupting the clock, so the world seems closed to the possibility of God's intervention in the natural course of events.

More recent discoveries, however, have changed that

perspective and now the mechanical metaphor seems inadequate: "Though there are some Newtonian clocks, most of [the world] is made of clouds."[13] The "cloud" metaphor carries the idea that the pieces of the world fit together loosely, with lots of flexibility and even unpredictability. A cloud can be redirected with a puff of wind and end up in a completely different place. The systems that make up the world as we understand it now are so sensitive and interwoven with each other that slight changes in one area can bring about larger changes elsewhere. This understanding is called "chaos theory" and is often summarized, not entirely inaccurately, by saying that a butterfly beating its wings in Brazil can cause a hurricane in Japan. Furthermore, the world as disclosed by science is no longer seen as a tight system of cause and effect. The deeply quantum character of events introduces an element of unpredictability and even freedom to the world. "In unprecedented circumstances, totally unanticipated things may happen, giving rise in those events which, because of their unexpected character, we might call miracles," Polkinghorne said. And miracles, along with "answers to prayer" occur as "insights into a deeper divine rationality."[14]

Seeking that deeper divine rationality keeps prayer from being an exercise in magic. Miracles that occurred in Scripture did not occur just to astonish people. They occurred to reveal the deeper purposes of God in the world. Even with miracles, which always involve the particular circumstances of a situation, there is a consistency to what God does.

This is impossible to quantify and predict, which is why it becomes such an important question for scientists whose lives are concerned with quantifiable and predictable results. As the world continues to create itself through the unfolding patterns in nature, there is divine interaction with creation. That is an entirely different view from God as the uninvolved clockmaker who set things in motion and then stepped away to let it unfold on its own; it is also different from God seen as a super Santa Claus granting wishes to good boys and girls. "Christian theology must always seek to find a middle way between two extreme and unacceptable pictures of God's relationship to creation," Polkinghorne said.[15]

In prayer, "we are offering our room for maneuver in bringing about the future to be taken and used by God, together with the divine providential room for maneuver, to produce the greatest possible good effect."[16] That means aligning our wills with God's will. When several people commit to aligning their wills with God's will, that collective spirit acts like laser light, he said, where the light is very intense because the many waves of light work together in the same wave pattern (the crests of the waves are the same, and so are the troughs). The mutual alignment makes the laser beam more powerful. All the waves are in step. When they are not in step, the waves and troughs cancel each other out and the result is a weak beam. "In prayer we are seeking a laser-like coherence between human will and divine will, and when those two wills are aligned, I believe things can happen that would not happen if they were at cross-purposes."[17]

The laser analogy fits with Polkinghorne's view that all things are linked throughout the universe. Collaboration has consequences. Since the world is open-ended and still being created, we participate with God in bringing about the future when we pray. That in itself reveals an extraordinary relationship between the God of creation and those he created. "It is an astonishing thought that our preferences should play a part in determining what is to be achieved through creation, but that is part of the loving respect of a Father for his children," he said. "Loving respect is due also from children to their Father."[18]

However, just because we believe our wills are aligned with God's, there are no guarantees. The apostle Paul prayed repeatedly for whatever his "thorn in the flesh" was to be removed, to no avail. It often appears that petitionary prayer simply does not work. In fact, studies have been unable to show, at least in the case of healing, that petitionary prayer has an influence at all on the medical outcomes. "There is so much that God might do, from curing our young neighbor who has liver cancer to bringing peace to a war-torn country, but which doesn't actually come about. No one can talk about prayer with any honesty without facing the mystery of individual destiny."[19] In the examples of the deaths of David Watson and John Robinson, "I wouldn't be so crude as to say, 'If only more people had prayed, they would have been healed.' When we pray we have creator/creature collaboration. The outcome doesn't depend on how many votes were on each side. Death is part of God's will in an evolving world."

Stating what is on our minds when we pray is important, says Polkinghorne. "We must pray in right spirit, even though we might have misplaced motives at first, and say what's in our hearts," he said. "So much of life is sliding down a knife's edge. There is an element of submission in prayer."

Prayer is not a way to persuade God to come around to our way of thinking. Rather it is a way for us to get our will aligned with God's and then invest in a course of action. Jesus, to take the most dramatic prayer in all of history, wanted to be spared his crucifixion, and told God as much. Stating it is a way of committing ourselves to it, Polkinghorne says. "In a similar way, we have to commit ourselves to what it is that we really want, to what is our heart's desire," he said. "Prayer is a very serious business." Prayer is a way for us to state what we truly value. Often, prayer is what spurs us to action. It's not enough to pray for our neighbor who is lonely, he said. Prayer in the right spirit will move us to act on that neighbor's loneliness and do something about it.[20]

Keith Ward, an Anglican priest who taught at Oxford for many years and also writes about science and faith, views prayer in much the same way as Polkinghorne. When we state our desires and our requests, we articulate what is in the deep recesses of our selves, which is the first step in motivating us to help bring about that desired future. "But if God knows and responds to all things, then God will know and respond to human prayers," Ward says. "The forms of divine response will be limited by the constraints of nature and freedom. But it seems reasonable to think that our attempts to become more conscious of God, to discern the divine will, and to ask for divine help will open the world of which we are part to divine providential action in ways that might not otherwise have existed." Prayer is the cooperation of human and divine that helps bring about a redemptive future.[21]

Prayer also addresses one of the root issues in the relationship of humanity and God. "I often think how transformed our lives would be if we really, deep down within us, fully believed that God loves us," Polkinghorne said. "If our trust was full and steadfast, rather than feeble and perhaps fleeting, what different people we should be. I think that is my heart's desire, to know the love of God."[22] If we really grasped the love of God for us, we would see a deep tranquility of life, he said. We would know more peace and less anxiety. Polkinghorne, by his own admission, does not have that knowledge – yet. "I am not a deeply tranquil person," he said. "Sometimes, during the Eucharist or contemplative prayer, I get these shafts of light through the clouds. I have more of a fluctuating life. I am not immune from desert experiences. Those periods have their role. That's when I wonder if it's too good to be true, and hang on by the skin of my teeth."

Many Christians throughout history have acknowledged such doubts, from the psalmist, to the apostle Paul, to Augustine, to St Francis, to Luther, to Mother Teresa, and to countless reflective Christians today. "They all had their flaws," Polkinghorne said, "and they all brought their flaws to God."

Sometimes we come to prayer tired, lonely, anxious, angry, frustrated, sad, bitter. Some might feel embarrassed to bring such feelings to God in prayer. But Polkinghorne believes this is exactly what the psalmist did on many occasions and what Jesus was doing when he prayed in the Garden. "When we pray we are in the presence of the God 'to whom all hearts are open, all desires known, and from whom no secrets are hidden.' Before this God there is neither room nor need for any pretence. We do not have to keep up pious appearances. The God of truth expects us to be absolutely honest with him."[23] Our hearts are healed when they are exposed to this loving God, and he is not offended by anger or frustration in the face of tragedy.

All of this came to the forefront again for Polkinghorne six years after he had retired from Queens' College, when his wife Ruth began having trouble with her eyesight in 2002. Medical tests showed that her blood was becoming dangerously thick. More blood tests revealed a rare form of leukemia. The family prayed together, primarily for peace and a sense that she was being sustained by God. "While I prayed continually for Ruth, I realized that God frequently allows nature to take its course," Polkinghorne said.

Chemotherapy slowed the disease for two years, a time the two of them enjoyed traveling to visit children and grandchildren. They celebrated their fiftieth wedding anniversary, spending the day with their family. Each of their three children made a brief speech and presentation to the parents, focusing on different memories of their life together. "It was a happy, joyous day, unsullied by sadness. We were unaware of the cloud that was hanging over it," Polkinghorne recalled.

Just before Ruth's disease returned, John read that the average survival rate was four to five years. "I was smitten by that," he said. "I thought the chemo would continue and save her. I truly was bowled over by this knowledge. When it came back, it was the very scenario I had read about."

Ruth's health quickly deteriorated and she began needing regular transfusions. It was clear that her time was short and for a few days she received visitors for brief periods of time. A skillful musician, Ruth had been part of a weekly workshop that made stringed instruments. She had labored happily for nearly four years to make the cello that she played in community orchestras. During the years of her illness she began making a violin for their beloved granddaughter Elizabeth, but, as it neared completion, it became clear that she would be unable to varnish the instrument. Members of the workshop completed that final task for her.

On Sunday, Mothering Sunday, the day of Ruth and John's fifty-first wedding anniversary, the family gathered around Ruth's hospital bed, coming alongside for the last time. "Here, Lizzy, this is for you," Ruth said, as she handed over the finished instrument with a new coat of varnish. Elizabeth, barely thirteen, understood the significance. It was Ruth's last conscious act. "We were all tearful. It was deeply moving. I saw it as one of God's well-engineered coincidences," John said. That night Ruth slipped in and out of consciousness. For two days the family sat alongside. John leaned in and whispered in her ear, "I'm here, darling. God's here. Come unto me all who are heavy laden, and I will give you rest." Within moments her lips turned blue, the family joined hands and, as John prayed, committed her into the hands of God.

"It was the transformation of suffering – both awful and glorious," he said. "I was sorry she didn't stay longer. I don't think that if we had more faith she would have been healed," he said. "She didn't think that, either. I do wish I had talked more with her about this. I might have made misjudgments about not speaking of it. But you're reacting all the time and are caught up in what is happening. Her healing was in our acceptance and in being present with her."

The flowers from her funeral were displayed a few days

later at church for Easter Sunday. For John Polkinghorne, this was an important symbol of that great Christian hope that he sometimes thinks is too good to be real – the hope of destiny beyond death, the hope that death is not the end, but is rather the gate of life. "Death is real, and it brings about a real separation from a much-loved companion, but it is not the ultimate reality," he said.[24] There is *always* more to the story.

CHAPTER FOUR

Regime Change

The tiny village of Blean sits on a tract of land in the south-eastern part of England, a few miles up the hill from Canterbury in the county of Kent. Natural springs run just below the surface and as a result not much can be developed on that land. Few have heard of Blean, sitting as it does in the long shadow of the medieval city of Canterbury. Blean has a population of about 3,000, some spectacular gardens, orchards, and an active village citizenry. It was built along a Roman salt road that connected the port city of Whitstable to Canterbury, and from certain vantage points one can see the nearby University of Kent and the famed Canterbury Cathedral.

Blean has one house of worship – a thirteenth-century Anglican church on the edge of town, incorporating the ruins of an ancient Roman villa. The old church has a graveyard going back to the 1600s, its tombstones raked by time and now standing at varying angles. The stone and brick building blends into the wooded surroundings, and is not visible from any well-traveled street. Joggers and cyclists are the only locals that see the church, as they pass by on a narrow path.

Canterbury Cathedral, by contrast, dates back to the sixth century and has been the site of innumerable historical events, including the murder of one of its many famous archbishops – Thomas Becket. It stands out as the center of activity in that bustling city. It was the destination of the travelers chronicled in Chaucer's *The Canterbury Tales*, and the setting for T. S. Eliot's play *Murder in the Cathedral* as well as the movie, *Becket*, starring Richard Burton and Peter O'Toole. There is a security gate where visitors pay a significant fee to enter its grounds, and the cathedral's spires are visible for miles. The sanctuary holds thousands and is one of the stops on most tourist excursions to the city.

The Blean church holds a congregation of about 200 and remains unlocked from sunrise to evening; a welcoming, cool shelter for people walking or biking on the nearby footpaths, and for students at the University of Kent, about a mile away, who need a study break. Visitors often leave notes of thanks in the guest registry.

The vicar of Blean between 1984 and 1986 – the one clergy person for the area above Canterbury – was John Polkinghorne, who served humbly and without fanfare. In contrast, Archbishop Robert Alexander Kennedy Runcie, who had also studied at Westcott, served down the road at Canterbury. Runcie presided over the wedding of Prince Charles and Lady Diana in 1981 and proposed an ambitious reconciliation with the Roman Catholic Church in 1989.

After finishing at seminary and serving as an associate priest, just two short years after he left the world of physics at the University of Cambridge – a university as well known as Canterbury Cathedral – Revd Polkinghorne began knocking on doors in Blean, getting to know the people in his parish.

His reputation as a world-class physicist preceded him and he used it to his advantage. For those who mistrusted or had no use for science, he had a word of encouragement. For those who mistrusted or had no use for religion, he had an equally encouraging word. In fact, he set about to ask the residents of Blean to lose their fear of either, and to embrace both science *and* religion.

Some began attending church as a result of Polkinghorne knocking on their doors and talking to them about God. "You can do this yourself, you know," he told one potential parishioner after engaging him in conversation about God. "You can think about these spiritual things." The next Sunday that man was to be seen in church.

The entire village of Blean was Polkinghorne's parish so he knocked on all the doors of the villagers – he spoke to people who were angry at religion, atheists, members of other faiths. Everyone answered their doors at some point only to see the Revd John Polkinghorne, ex-mathematical physicist, stopping by to see if he could engage those at home in conversation. "If a Jewish person in the parish just lost her husband, John was the first one knocking on her door offering her help," said a parishioner. And he was never turned away.

For Polkinghorne, the best part of being the vicar of Blean was being able to participate in the life of the small community. Because he was the vicar of the only church in the area, he got involved in the village flower show, the children's costume contest, and even the raffle put on by elderly groups. "As I wandered around town I could say hello to anyone I wanted," he said, recalling this time with great pleasure.

At baptisms and weddings he told individuals and families he was glad they wanted the acknowledgment of the church during these memorable times, but it meant taking vows in the presence of God. He loved explaining what those vows entailed. At one baptism on a typically cold English winter morning, he poured the water into the baptistry, with the family and congregation standing around the concrete bowl. The baptistry was cold, however, and the water was room temperature, so when the water hit the bowl a cloud of fog erupted, looking very much like steam. "The parents were convinced I was going to scald their baby," Polkinghorne said. "So for the entire service I kept my own hand in the water to show that it was not too hot."

Weddings gave him the chance to explain to couples – especially those who were not part of a faith tradition – that matrimony was a lifetime commitment, and that the biggest changes would come when they had children. "I got to be involved in people's lives at their significant points," he said. At funerals, if he didn't know the person who had died, he would try to find out details so he could make the service personal. "I had to find out something about old Joe so I could make it meaningful," he said. "I also tried to give some hope, and tell them that nothing good was lost in the Lord. It gave me a chance to say something about Christian hope."

Village life differed greatly from what he knew best – the college community. College life involves a restricted group limited to mostly faculty and students, and for much of the year, including Christmas, they weren't even in town. "That kind of community doesn't exhaust the richness of human varieties and diversity," he said and then added, perhaps with some hyperbole, "But a town does."

Serving in Blean was not uniformly pleasant, however. Six or more times a year the vicar was expected to speak at assemblies of elementary school children. "I don't remember how six-year-olds think," he said. "I sweated over those far more than sermons for my congregation. One time I told about Jesus the Good Shepherd and drew some figures on the chalkboard that eventually became sheep. I was quite pleased with myself that day."

If any in the congregation were concerned about not being able to understand a sermon preached by a man who had been taught by the great physicists of the twentieth century, those fears subsided quickly. "We were never intimidated by John's intelligence or reputation as this world-renowned scientist," said one parishioner. "He was one of us from the very beginning. Although, when I try to read his books I can't get past the first page!" And not everyone, of course, was even aware of their new priest's worldwide reputation in the physics community. A newspaper reporter, assigned to do a story on the new priest in town, asked Polkinghorne if there was anything unusual about him that might be of interest to the newspaper's readers. Polkinghorne told the reporter that he was a Fellow of the Royal Society, a position that no other clergyman in the nation held. The reporter replied, "Royal Society of what?"

The vicar of Blean kept his sermons to ten minutes, and rarely regaled his congregation with anecdotes, cute stories about his family life, or even about his own rather extraordinary life experience. He stuck to the lectionary and explicated his text succinctly and with precision. An Anglican church official attending one of his services said that the sermon was "brisk, but a reverent brisk." Polkinghorne laughed recalling the incident – "I want that on my tombstone."

Years after Polkinghorne's experience in Blean, a parishioner still remembered one of his first sermons where he used the example of why the kettle of water was boiling, mentioned in Chapter One. "He told us to think about science and religion in light of this question," she said. "It made perfect sense. Science can easily answer the question of why the water is boiling. So can religion. But neither one tells the whole story on its own."

In the mornings, Polkinghorne would write in the house provided by the parish, a pleasant two-story brick dwelling that was a five-minute walk down a gravel road from the church. During his time in the village he wrote one of his most successful books, *One World: The Interaction of Science and Theology*. The book argues that we live in one world, and that science and theology study different aspects of this one world in order to understand it better – the story of the teapot, writ large. In the afternoons he put down his pen and went to call on people in his parish.

His greatest experiences as the vicar of Blean, however, were the frequent but never familiar celebrations of the Eucharist with the people at his church. After all the discussion, all the reading and debate about God, all the books and all the writing, all the theories and equations, for Polkinghorne, the real moment of truth came in the mystical sharing of the elements of Christ's blood and body. In that act the central tenets of Christian belief are reaffirmed: the death and resurrection of Jesus. "It is a special form of encounter with our risen Lord, an invisible, fluctuating presence," he said. "There is an importance of regularity, of showing commitment and obedience to Jesus who said to his disciples, 'Do this.'"

Before he went to seminary, Polkinghorne had felt some frustration that, as a non-ordained person, he could not celebrate the Eucharist for a congregation, but could only assist in the administration of the sacrament. As a child he was unable to even receive the elements, because he hadn't gone through the church's confirmation classes. "My parents were concerned I would have too many distractions from my studies if I took a night a week for confirmation," he said. "It was my parents' protective actions from having just one surviving child." He was confirmed when he was seventeen. "It was unsatisfactory to not participate. I had a sense of incompleteness."

Since the experience of receiving the elements was so profound in his own personal faith, he wanted to help others share that experience. In Blean, every Sunday and every Wednesday there was opportunity to extend the elements of this mystical experience to members of a congregation willing to accept the Mystery. Some brought their children with them to the altar for a prayer of blessing. They approached the altar, knelt before the scientist who believed in things he could not see – quarks, gluons, God, love – and watched as he handed them the wafer and cup and said "This is the body of Christ, broken for you. This is the blood of Christ, shed for you." This, for Polkinghorne, was the best part of being a priest – the reward for having walked away from physics.

The church had a custom of having special Eucharistic times for healing. At these times members of the congregation could come to the altar to receive the laying on of hands with prayer and to seek God's deliverance from various afflictions – physical, financial, emotional, even representational, where a person would receive this ministry on behalf of the predicament of another. The church also celebrated a Requiem Eucharist each month, where members of the congregation could remember those who had died during that month, or whose anniversaries of death occurred during that month. Whatever else may be said during the Eucharist, the central message is that "the Lord is here." In Polkinghorne's view, this is how the church speaks to itself through its history, and points beyond itself. The experience both remembers the past and calls forth the Spirit of God, an act that has the character of the already of the past and the not yet of the future.[1]

Polkinghorne's thinking on the importance of the Eucharist was shaped in part by the Greek Orthodox theologian John Zizioulas. "In the Eucharistic assembly God's Word reaches man and creation not from outside, as in the Old Testament, but as 'flesh' – from inside our own existence, as part of creation," Zizioulas wrote in his book *Being as Communion*.[2] The dwelling place of God is not in a person's mind as rational thought, or in the soul as a mystical experience, Zizioulas said, "but as communion within a community." Christ becomes known as truth because, through the Eucharist, the community becomes truth itself.[3] "Truth is not imposed upon us but springs up from our midst," he said, and "comes clearly from another world… Truth liberates by placing beings in communion."[4]

According to Zizioulas, scientists like Polkinghorne had already been experiencing a type of communion in their laboratories. "The scientist who is a Church member will be able to recognize that he is carrying out a para-eucharistic work," he wrote. "The Eucharistic conception of truth can thus liberate man from his lust to dominate nature, making him aware that the Christ-truth exists for the life of the whole cosmos… all creation and not just to humanity."[5]

The bread and wine of the Eucharist are both representations of nature and of human labor. "They represent the drawing together, in the action of the Eucharist, of the fruits of nature and the fruits of human work and skill in the total offering of creation," Polkinghorne said. "The Eucharistic gifts unite nature and human culture... In these ways, the bread and wine that we receive at Communion are integrated into a profound and all-embracing context, which offers us also some insight into how it is that these gifts become for us truly the means by which we receive the body and blood of Christ."[6]

Polkinghorne encountered some people in Blean who believed in God enough that they prayed occasionally when they needed something, such as good health and weather, and maybe the winning number in the National Lottery, but they didn't seem to be on that same quest for knowledge and truth that he experienced in his scientific pursuits, or during his theological training in academia. Many people he encountered there had more of a folk religion than a vigorous relationship with the Creator of the world. "I do not despise folk religion, though I am saddened by its shallowness and its misapprehensions about the nature of God," he said.[7]

One aspect of that nature that he wanted to communicate clearly was that the gospel really is true – that God, the One who started it all billions of years ago, wanted to be in direct relationship with his creation. Jesus, the incarnation of God, lived among us, was crucified for showing that the traditional systems of greed and power were not the only options, and came back from the dead to continue to reveal the more excellent way to live. That kind of belief doesn't come easily for many people – especially the part about the resurrection. And one might assume that it would be even more difficult for a scientist to believe it.

But the scientific training of Polkinghorne already

prepared him to expect the unexpected. The twentieth century had been full of surprises for physicists from the revelation that Newton had got it wrong and needed to be updated to the strange world of the quantum where electrons might seem to behave as if they had free will. "If science has taught us anything, it's that the world always surprises us," he said. "If we cannot foretell what we shall find when we enter a new physical regime then it is to be anticipated that our encounter with God will not always accord with prior expectation," he continued. "A scientific approach would always seek first to accept and evaluate the phenomena, whatever they might be, and allow experience rather than so-called 'reason' (which here, in fact, is often a euphemism for paucity of imagination) to set the agenda."[8]

Polkinghorne had already wrestled with the idea that light is both a wave and a particle, two fundamentally contradictory viewpoints. Acceptance that the simple reality of something as familiar as light required deep paradox serves as a preparation for wrestling with the central Christian belief that Jesus is both human and divine, that he lived and died and lives again. Scientists hold on to perplexing paradoxes all the time. "We live in a subtle world and both science and theology need to be subtle in their accounts of it," Polkinghorne said.[9]

As a priest, Polkinghorne is motivated to believe that Jesus lived, died, and lives again. The book of Isaiah in the Old Testament speaks of prophets. Is Jesus just one of those prophets, or more than that? "Jesus had a historically unusual life," Polkinghorne said. "He was greeted by crowds with high expectations. But it all falls apart and his followers run away. He suffers a painful and shameful death, and appears to be rejected by God. On the face of it, you would think 'Here is another messianic pretender who got his comeuppance.' If that was it, we would have never heard from him again."

N. T. Wright, the former bishop of Durham, echoes this

view. "Take away the stories of Jesus' birth, and all you lose is four chapters of the gospels. Take away the resurrection and you lose the entire New Testament, and most of the second century fathers as well."[10] But can a scientist, for whom skepticism is a virtue, believe that Jesus rose from the dead?

Jesus was compelling as an authoritative preacher proclaiming that the kingdom of God had arrived. He taught and embodied a selfless love, used the imaginative language of parables to describe this new kingdom, questioned the values and priorities of the dominant culture, welcomed the outcasts, healed those whose paths he crossed, became angry at stubbornness and hypocrisy, warned about judgment, and said things that were hard to accept. These traits, however, don't set him that far apart from other religious figures in history, such as Moses, Mohammed, and the Buddha. Those three lived to an old age and were surrounded by devoted followers who vowed to carry on the message of their leader. "From the point of view of the history of religions, what is unique about Jesus is not his life but his death," Polkinghorne said.[11] Jesus' life is cut short after three years of ministry, an apparent failure, abandoned by his followers.

The humiliation of the crucifixion was the final act in yet one more delusional man's life. There is no mystery why his followers fled. But the very followers who deserted him were soon energized in their own ministries, claiming that Jesus was raised from the dead. "On the truth or falsehood of that belief turns the whole Christian understanding of God and God's purposes in Jesus of Nazareth," he said.[12] It's as surprising and as unusual now to believe such a thing as it was in the first century. "But it is the pivot point – the clear indication of God," he said. "I could still believe in the Divine Mind and Purpose without it, but the essence of Christianity pivots on the resurrection. Quite a lot of people might think I'm mistaken. I'm not worried about that."

There is evidence for the resurrection, Polkinghorne says, that makes him – the hardnosed, skeptical scientist – think it actually occurred. In any inquiry, scientific or otherwise, one should ask at least these two questions: "Is there evidence?" and "Does it make sense?" Resurrection, as opposed to resuscitation, is the transformation of the life of one who died into a life everlasting, no longer confined to a history where everyone dies. The evidence, Polkinghorne says, leads him to think that something happened between Good Friday and Pentecost. The disciples, demoralized and terrified at his death, dramatically reversed course and became confident in their newly risen leader, even if it resulted in their own deaths. There were witnesses to the risen Christ, whose varying accounts had him in the garden near his tomb, in the upper room with his disciples, on the shore cooking breakfast, and on the road talking with strangers headed to Emmaus. In all these reported cases his appearance was unexpected and often there was an initial difficulty in recognizing the risen Christ before realizing who was there. These accounts differ in details from the accounts of the crucifixion, which were essentially identical. Accounts of Jesus' empty tomb are in all four Gospels, and the first to know about the resurrection were women.

This, says Polkinghorne, gives these accounts the ring of truth. Women had very low status in that society and were legally unreliable. But their accounts were repeated and believed. If one was making up statements to manufacture credibility, women would be the last witnesses one would call on. "Without its having happened, it could be said, Jesus would never have been heard of after such a dismal end to his life," Polkinghorne said.[13]

But does it make sense? Yes, says Polkinghorne. It makes perfect sense that God did not abandon the one person who was totally committed to the divine will of God. It makes sense that acceptance of the suffering of the cross brings victory over all other destructive powers. It makes sense that the life, death, and new life of Jesus shows us that there is a destiny beyond what we experience on this earth. This can't be proven, and it certainly can't be completely understood – but then neither can light. If it happened, it carries all the significance in the world about who Jesus is and how he taught us to live. If it didn't happen, Christianity is at best a morality tale and at worst a fairy tale. "No one can convince the skeptical against their will, but there is both significant historical and theological motivation for the belief," he said.[14]

The evidence is adequate for Polkinghorne. "I believe that the resurrection of Jesus makes sense in this way because it fulfils three conditions: 1) it was not fitting that his life should end in total failure; 2) it was not fitting that God should abandon the one man who wholly put his trust in him; 3) it is fitting that our deep hopes that death does not have the last word about human significance should be vindicated."[15] There is motivating evidence and interpretation, which leads to a judgment you have to make. "The judgment amounts to a kind of leap, which makes it sound irrational." But scientists made leaps about quarks and gluons. About relativity. About the Big Bang. And about particles and waves.

"If Jesus was raised from the dead, there was something unique about him. And the resurrection is the point on which my belief turns," he said. "Apparently his life did not end in failure. The most compelling thing about Jesus is not his teaching, but his resurrection. His teaching had precedents. There had to be more than Gandhi's reverence for his Sermon on the Mount. God's head was on the block on Good Friday. Ultimately, everyone must make a movement of judgment. Atheists make a judgment, too."

If a person cannot believe that the resurrection occurred, that's a perfectly understandable position, he said. "Science tells us that the dead stay dead," he said. "The resurrection is a first

– a great new act of God. If there ever was a miracle, that was it." He wrote, "No one could suppose that a dead man came alive, never to die again, through some clever divine exploitation of quantum theory or chaotic dynamics."[16]

Some scholars propose that the resurrection was an idea that believers invented years after the event, because the cause of Jesus continued beyond his death. Since the cause was life after death, one could metaphorically say that Jesus was still alive, and then eventually lose the metaphor altogether and speak of an actual historical resurrection. Polkinghorne will have none of this. Furthermore, the accounts of the disciples themselves are hardly consistent with such an emaciated concept of resurrection.

Just as theories that include quarks make more sense to physicists than theories that don't – a deep insight that the skeptical agnostic Weinberg embraced with vigor – theories that include the resurrection make more sense to Christians than those that don't. "The resurrection is not only the vindication of Jesus. It is also the vindication of God: that he did not abandon the one man who wholly trusted himself to him. Moreover, we begin to see here some glimmer of a divine response to the problem of evil. If Good Friday testifies to the reality of the power of evil, Easter Day shows that the last word lies with God."[17] The resurrection is also the wellspring of ultimate hope for humanity. "We shall all die with our lives to a greater or lesser extent incomplete, unfulfilled, unhealed. Yet there is a profound and widespread human intuition that in the end all will be well... The resurrection is the beginning of God's great act of redemptive transformation, the seed from which the new creation begins to grow."[18]

But not even all Christians can accept this thinking. Polkinghorne sees skepticism about the resurrection present in Christian circles, not just atheistic science circles. "Some in modern Christianity discount the resurrection," he said.

"That's a big mistake. The most important statement we can make is that Jesus lives. Not just in concept, but is really alive. The resurrection is the unique status of Jesus. It is a decisive new act of God."

Polkinghorne knows how he is perceived when he makes these claims. Some see him the way he sees Mormons – chasing absurd and implausible ideas. He realizes that believing in the resurrection of Jesus is a strange idea, but it is not as strange as believing what Mormons believe. "They are wonderful people, and Ruth and I were struck by their extraordinary kindness when we visited Utah and read their book of Mormon." But believing in the resurrection is a long way from believing in the finding of golden plates, as described in the Book of Mormon, he said. "Go back to motivated beliefs," he stressed. "Mormons are nice and educated, but with extraordinary and strange beliefs. After reading the Book of Mormon I have higher regard for the Bible. It's easier to take the Bible seriously than that manufactured pastiche that wasn't very well written."

The resurrection certainly stretches a rational mind, especially the skeptical mind of a scientist. But the idea of miracles of any sort is similarly troublesome. How can a scientist believe in, let alone explain, a miracle? Science can't say that miracles won't occur. Such a claim goes beyond the purview of science and is essentially equivalent to the claim that there cannot be a God. Science can say only that miracles aren't to be expected and should be examined very critically before being accepted at face value. Besides, miracles also create theological problems. Do miracles reveal that God is showing off? Or that he can be convinced to do something if enough people pound on his door? The problem presented by miracles is whether God is consistent.

"It is theologically incredible that God acts as a kind of celestial conjurer, doing occasional tricks to astonish people but most of the time not bothering," Polkinghorne said. "Such

a capricious notion of divine action is totally unacceptable...
By their nature, miracles are unique events and not recurrent
phenomena," which puts them outside the scope of scientific
explanation. They can't be repeated in a laboratory.[19] What
constitutes a miracle isn't just something out of the ordinary –
an odd event, "such as would be the sudden materialization in
Trafalgar Square of a twelve-foot-high statue of Nelson made of
chocolate," he wrote.[20] The event must have some significance
and meaning. "Miracles must be perceptions of a deeper
rationality than that which we encounter in the every day,
occasions which make visible a more profound level of divine
activity. They are transparent moments in which the Kingdom
is found to be manifestly present."[21]

In the incident of the feeding of the 5,000, the only miracle
reported in all four Gospels, there is the event, and there is
the deeper glimpse into the divine. "If the point of that story
was 'Everyone should share,' that's very limp, and the point
would have been stated," he said. "But it's also a foretaste of the
messianic banquet and has Eucharistic overtones. It happened,
but it revealed something else." Miracles are not divine acts
against the laws of nature, which themselves are expressions
of God's will, but are revelations of the character of the divine
relationship to creation. "To be credible, miracles must convey a
deeper understanding than could have been obtained without
them."[22]

Word choice matters to Polkinghorne when discussing
miracles. Like most scientists who are people of faith, he
almost never uses words like "intervention". The preferred
word is "interaction," a term that has replaced "force" for
many contemporary physicists, who speak now of gravitational
interactions, rather than forces.[23]

Do miracles occur outside of established natural
laws? Polkinghorne points to superconductivity. Electrical
conduction is a common phenomenon that works consistently

most of the time; one common feature of such conduction is that the resistance of the metal causes it to heat up, and energy is lost. But at certain temperatures, in certain metals, things change suddenly and this resistance disappears. We call this superconductivity – current now flows freely. And, in certain superconductors, the presence of additional metals allows the superconduction to take place at much higher temperatures. (Scientists are working hard to find a superconductor that will work at room temperature, which would be a major technological breakthrough that would all but eliminate the waste heat generated by devices like computers and cellphones.)

The laws of nature don't change when a conductor turns into a superconductor, or when new metals are added to existing superconductors. But the consequences change in unexpected ways. "A regime changed, but not the laws themselves," he said. Polkinghorne sees Jesus' resurrection as a new regime, accompanied by new phenomena. "The uniqueness of the resurrection is in its singularity, which lies in its timing within history, as the foretaste of what awaits all of us – the restoration of unending life."

N. T. Wright sees the resurrection in much the same way. It is "not an absurd event within the old world, but the symbol and starting point of the new world." It's not just an odd event "within the world as it is, but the utterly characteristic, prototypical and foundational event within the world as it has begun to be... With Jesus of Nazareth there is not simply a new religious possibility, not simply a new ethic or a new way of salvation, but a new creation."[24]

This kind of intellectual commitment is not that difficult for a scientist to make, Polkinghorne argues. "People say that scientists are skeptical and doubt everything. That's simply absurd. If they doubted everything they would have no starting point."

Wright said that scientists can believe in the resurrection because the event "transcends but includes what we call history and what we call science... Insofar as I understand scientific method, when something turns up which doesn't fit the paradigm you're working with, one option at least, perhaps when all others have failed, is to change the paradigm, not to exclude everything you've known to that point but to include it within a larger whole."[25]

After two years as the vicar of Blean (1984–86), the University of Cambridge came calling on their old friend. Trinity Hall, a college within the system even older than Trinity College, was looking for a new Dean of the Chapel. Was he interested?

Polkinghorne returned to Cambridge for an interview. The job included directing worship in the chapel, being responsible for pastoral care over the College community, and being director of theological studies. The job also provided time for him to pursue his growing interest in writing. Leaving Blean was difficult. He had forged deep relationships in that small village. It was there he had responded to the vocational call that drew him away from Cambridge in the first place. But this new position combined both the academic and the priestly roles. It would let him be both a wave and a particle.

Church members were sad to see him go, of course. He had become a beloved figure in the tiny parish. And he and his wife Ruth were both sad to be leaving. But even Trinity Hall couldn't contain him for long. He was soon elected president of Queens' College, where he presided from 1989 until his retirement in 1996.

Decades later, in 2009, Polkinghorne returned to Blean for a weekend to counsel, preach, and celebrate the Eucharist with the congregation while the current vicar was on vacation. Families he had advised years before returned for counsel regarding their latest predicaments. A neighborhood garden party was ramped up into a community-wide event to celebrate his return. The news media were alerted.

On Sunday morning, Polkinghorne rose early, walked the gravel pathway to the edge of town as he had done twenty-five years before, and entered the church. A gentle, English-style rain had fallen the day before, and the remaining mist gave the building and its surroundings a soupy medieval cloak. A room in the back of the sanctuary held the vestments for him to wear and the Eucharist elements for him to dispense. It also held the icon that he had commissioned when he was the village vicar.

The icon portrayed the patron saints of the Blean church, Damian and Cosmus, two North African brothers who converted to Christianity in the third century, and were martyred for their new faith. They were Arab doctors who reportedly pioneered transplant surgery. Historical records include paintings of them sewing the leg of a black slave onto the body of a white prince who had lost a leg in battle. As vicar, Polkinghorne had commissioned Russian Orthodox monks known for painting icons in the traditional style to create one for Damian and Cosmus. The church brings it out for special occasions.

On this day, Polkinghorne, moving a bit slower than he had twenty-five years earlier, carried the icon to the front of the church and placed it under the bright blue and red stained glass windows that had been designed by a local artist. A nearby window, mostly clear, was speckled with mosaics of pieces of stained glass. The original windows had been smashed by dour Victorians rebelling against the opulence of Anglican churches. He noticed that the pipe organ had been moved from the front of the church to the rear – a colossal undertaking. It had taken years to disassemble the organ, store it while a new foundation was poured in the rear of the church, and then reassemble it at the back of the church. Moving the organ exposed tombs of Blean parishioners from the 1600s, some of whom had died while Isaac Newton was teaching at Cambridge. Moving the organ was a great idea. Its location in the front had blocked the view of the chancel for half the congregation.

Polkinghorne then prepared the table for the Eucharist as he had done so many times before. He arranged his papers at the pulpit. He would be preaching in less than an hour.

The choir and the organist arrived to rehearse. Other members gathered – word had spread that their celebrity priest was back in town. In came the former mayor of Canterbury, who served during Polkinghorne's time up the hill. Polkinghorne had been her chaplain. There was the chaplain to Rowan Williams, who became Archbishop of Canterbury in 2002. And there were the regular attendees, on whose doors he had knocked years before. He had visited them in hospital, married them, buried their family members, blessed them. Some had seen him recently on the BBC talking about a new C. S. Lewis exhibit. Others had seen him on the BBC discussing the ethics of embryonic stem cell research. Some had attended a recent lecture he gave at Oxford. Some brought with them books they wanted to discuss with him.

Polkinghorne returned to the rear of the church and gathered with four church members in white robes. They prayed briefly together and lined up, with Polkinghorne in the lead.

At 9.45 a.m. the sound of the church bell rolled across the countryside as it had for centuries, announcing to the village that the service was starting. At 10 a.m. the church was full. The organist launched the opening measures as he had so many times before. The congregation began to sing "Christ the Lord is Risen Today." The former mathematical physicist, now knighted, John Polkinghorne, dressed in a white robe with a green sash, led the procession, once more, to the altar.

CHAPTER FIVE

Here and There

John Polkinghorne is on his knees, a familiar pose for the man who has been a priest for three decades and a Christian for his entire life. He is not in worship this time, though. He's looking for a CD – a particular CD amid racks of discs of classical music on the shelves in his sitting room in Cambridge.

"Ah, here it is!" he exclaims. "I'll start with the Sanctus." He is listening to his favorite musical work, Bach's Mass in B Minor. Bach wrote pieces of this classic over three decades, and compiled it into a single mass in 1749, a year before he died. Music scholars consider the piece an enigma – a work written in Latin by a German Protestant that is too long for most religious services.

Johann Sebastian Bach was a man of few words who suffered from the deaths of loved ones throughout his life. His parents died when he was a child. Several of his children died, an experience all too familiar before modern medicine. His wife died in her thirties. And yet the music he wrote seems to usher listeners into the presence of God more than 250 years later.

The "Sanctus" (Latin for *holy*) is a hymn typically sung as a part of the Eucharistic Prayer. In the movement the vocalists sing "Holy, holy, holy is the Lord of Hosts. Hosanna in the highest. Blessed is He who comes in the name of the Lord." Polkinghorne listens once again to the familiar piece, smiling. During the *Symbolum Nicenum*, Bach's musical interpretation of the Nicene Creed, Polkinghorne's eyes close. His Gifford Lectures, published as *The Faith of a Physicist*, focused on this famous fourth-century creed but this interpretation meets with his full approval and he is clearly moved. As the strings and mournful tones move toward the part depicting the crucifixion, Polkinghorne puts his head down, seemingly afraid to witness Christ on the cross. At the sound of the trumpets and tympani soaring into the resurrection segment, he brightens, swaying with the proclamation that Christ rose from the dead and ascended to sit at the right hand of the Father.

"It's the music of heaven," he said, smiling. "It kindles in me hope."

Some years before, Polkinghorne had been interviewed on the radio in Australia. The host asked how he would like to end the interview, and he said to end it with the Sanctus section of the Mass. It's something of a theme song for Polkinghorne.

"My reaction to it is so strong," he said. "It's similar to how I react when I see the Van Eyck painting *The Adoration of the Lamb*, which portrays the worship of heaven. The first time I saw it I sat in front of it for at least twenty minutes. As Wordsworth said, art and music convey intimations of immortality."

Music moves people deeply and is one of the oldest expressions of human culture. It has long played some role in humankind's understanding of who they were. When Polkinghorne talks about God to people who don't believe – "I admit that it is hard for some to make the leap from physics to God" – music is a good intermediary step. From a physical, or scientific, perspective one can explain how music "happens"; sounds originate from vibrations – in vocal cords, or string made of nylon, horse hair, steel, or a dried animal skin drawn tightly across a hollow log. The vibrations move into the air and are carried by the molecules in the air, as they vibrate. These vibrations spread out from the source and eventually into the ear canals of listeners. Here they vibrate the tissues within the ear, sending an electrical signal to the brain, which decodes the signal and determines whether the sound is pleasant. That's music, at least one version of it. But of course, that's not the whole story.

"Your understanding is limited if all you know is the scientific reduction," Polkinghorne said. "Music is more than the release of neurosensors in the brain. There is timeless mystery to music. It's central to the world of metaphysics."

Polkinghorne first heard Bach's Mass in B Minor when he was an undergraduate student, at a concert at King's College in Cambridge with Ruth in the orchestra.

"The crucifixion section portrays a life completely spent," he said. "Then there is a sudden burst of sound. I can't listen to it without thinking that Bach believed in the resurrection, and that this was an expression of his faith. That's part of its power."

The beauty of the Mass is difficult to explain, though. "There is an economy, an elegance, a depth, that aesthetic philosophers have difficulty describing," he said. "But the economy and elegance are not the total explanation."

There are simply some things that science can't do. At least not yet. The Mass is, in some deep and incomprehensible sense, a *Creation*. Had Bach not existed, it wouldn't have been created. It was a work that emerged as Bach's initiative. He gathered the elements of music together into this synthetic, creative expression. That's different from a scientific discovery.

"The theory of general relativity would have eventually been discovered – although in a more piecemeal manner – had Einstein not discovered it," Polkinghorne said. "The same goes for gravity. Beautiful patterns were seen within a structure. They're discovered, but that's different from creative discovery. Art is not repeatable in that same way." Only Bach knows all that went into creating the Mass in B Minor. Only he could have done it quite that way. No one, not even Bach himself, knows all of the "Whys" that went into creating that piece. Musicologists can tell us *how* he did it, what methods, what traditions, what influences he borrowed from, over how many years. But not *why* it was done this way.

Consider another remarkable creation – the universe. Scientists can now tell us how the universe came into being, through the Big Bang some 14 billion years ago. What they can't do is tell us the meaning and the purpose of the universe. "Science doesn't say anything beyond what *is* and should be," Polkinghorne said. "That doesn't mean that questions of value and meaning aren't significant. That's why science on its own fails to be satisfying. It is self-limiting. What makes a great piece of music or art can't be answered by science. It is manifestly false to say that science answers all of the big questions."

Beauty can be experienced in other ways than art or music, too, says Polkinghorne. There is beauty and elegance in mathematical equations. It may take some training to see this beauty, but then that is also true for learning to appreciate Bach. And, just as many pieces of music are not beautiful, so some equations can be ugly. He remembers thinking about this as he sat in a lecture hall listening to Paul Dirac explain quantum theory. The world-famous Dirac would be on most physicists' short list of the most brilliant – and most eccentric – scientists in the last century. In a large lecture hall Dirac would put a piece of chalk on one part of the chalk tray, and another piece on another part of the tray, and tell the students that in the everyday world, a piece of chalk is *here*, and a piece of chalk is *there*. But in the quantum world, the chalk is *partly* here and *partly* there. It's elsewhere, too. Probably.

Dirac considered it profoundly important to have equations with beauty in them. If the equation was ugly, where things didn't quite fit, then it might not be a fatal equation, but it was an equation that didn't work. Mathematicians, oddly enough, generally agree on what is beautiful and what is ugly, Polkinghorne said.

Dozens of students would fit in the lecture hall where Dirac taught. But visiting professors at Cambridge crowded in as well, just to listen to the great man who had made discoveries of historic significance. Dirac didn't entertain; he used no rhetorical tricks, but logically laid out his thought process. "Listening to him was like ingesting an element of a Bach fugue," Polkinghorne said. "He talked about some of his discoveries, but never bragged about his role – unlike many others." Dirac used a long chalkboard when he lectured, filling it so often that he had to repeatedly clean it to continue. Occasionally Polkinghorne would be in the foyer of the lecture hall talking with his classmates when Dirac, a tall, thin, distinguished figure in a black teaching robe and hair curled at the edges, would sweep through the hallway, rendering those nearby silent. "I knew at the time that I was in the presence of greatness," Polkinghorne said.

In later years they would be colleagues, teacher and student now on the same team. But that didn't make the great mathematician any more approachable than when Polkinghorne was a student. "There was not a lot of natural give and take with him," he said. "He had a single-minded and literal view of things, and may have even been autistic."

Physics culture is replete with stories of the eccentricities of its geniuses – Newton forgetting to get any sleep for three days and then wondering why simple math was getting so hard, Einstein reading the newspaper in a neighbor's house, unaware that he had come home to the wrong address, George Gamow scaring everyone with his motorcycle, Richard Feynman breaking into the top secret safes at Los Alamos and leaving messages for military security. The Dirac stories – and there are many – revolve around his social awkwardness and inability to make small talk. Polkinghorne remembers being at a conference with Dirac, and trying to chat with him at a seaside barbecue. England had recently converted its temperature measurement, so Polkinghorne commented on how hot it was, and that he hadn't quite gotten used to the shift from Fahrenheit to Celsius. Dirac, missing the point of Polkinghorne's "get to know you" comment, said, "It's very simple – you subtract 32 and multiply by 5/9ths."

"Well, I knew *that*," Polkinghorne recalled, laughing. "I was just commenting on the heat. But he was that literal."

Another time several of the world's great mathematicians were in the tea room at the Cavendish Laboratory, a building best known for Watson and Crick's discoveries about DNA's double helix. Some of the mathematicians around the tables were Nobel Laureates. They were discussing quantum mechanics, which was just about completed after a half-century of amazing discoveries that seemed to follow one after the other, like the hit songs of The Beatles. "In a very straightforward way, Dirac said that its development came about at a time when second-rate people did first-rate work," Polkinghorne said. "That was an amazing thing to say in the presence of such distinguished people, some of whom he was referring to!"

Whether it's music, art, mathematics, or faith, scientific discussion takes us only so far. "There are very important areas of experience that we value that can't be explained in scientific terms," Polkinghorne said. The "why" of the universe is one of those areas. To understand the magnitude of the universe and the questions of "how?" and "why?", Polkinghorne suggests conducting an experiment – a "thought experiment" of the kind for which Einstein was famous. You don't need a laboratory or a supercollider – just your imagination.

Imagine that you have been given a UCM – a Universe-Creating Machine. No such thing exists of course, despite the grandiose aspirations of the cosmologists. It's an experiment for your imagination. The UCM is an impressive piece of equipment. You are mesmerized by the number of knobs on it. Each knob specifies the scientific structure of the world you want to create. You're drawn to the gravity knobs because gravity seems so much simpler than some of the others that have names like "fine structure constant" and "electromagnetic coupling strength". The gravity knob has an "off" position, of course, because you get to choose whether you want gravity at all in this universe. If you do want gravity in your universe, what will be the nature of the gravity? Do you want the kind Isaac Newton discovered in our universe, or some other kind?

Once you've made the big decisions about gravity, you can twist the knob to adjust the strength of the gravity you desire. Do you want weak gravity, so the earth would be like the moon, where humans can cavort like children on a trampoline? Do you want gravity like it is now? Or do you want it much stronger, so it would be hard to get up out of your chair? You can design your universe any way you want. Feel free to try different levels and pay close attention to the results of each adjustment in your laboratory notebook as you create different universes.

How about another one of the big knobs on the machine – the one labeled "electromagnetism"? That's a pretty important one because electromagnetism is the force that holds atoms and molecules together, and we are made of atoms and molecules. In our universe electromagnetism is much stronger than gravity, but you can put it at whatever level you want. You can make it really weak and see how atoms go from being tiny, with the electron orbiting close to the nucleus, to very large, with the electrons orbiting far away and constantly getting unhooked from their nuclei.

There are other forces of nature that you'll have to get to as well, to make sure your universe functions in some sensible way. There is a so-called "strong" force that holds protons and neutrons together. You'll also have to decide if you want a vast universe like ours, with trillions of stars, or if you'd rather have something smaller and more manageable. The knobs go on and on, but eventually you'll get to all of them and adjust them to your desired levels. Now it's time to pull the big lever and see how it all turns out. It will take a few billion years (unless you turned the ultra-fast development knob all the way) but remember, this is a picture playing out in your imagination, or maybe on your computer.

Regardless of how you set the knobs on your UCM, your universe will develop in some sort of way, and it probably won't be very interesting. If you chose levels different from the universe we live in now, you'd see significant differences. For instance, if you made the force of gravity a tiny bit stronger, creatures – if there were any – would be shorter than you and me because it would be harder to grow tall. As you play with the UCM, you notice something quite surprising. Any time you change a setting so it is not the same as in our present universe, the universe that results is radically different from ours. Strangely, it appears there is no way to get creatures like us unless you leave the knobs all unchanged from the default settings that would produce this universe. The narrative of cosmic history that begins with the Big Bang some 14 billion years ago and leads to us does not look like a random and meandering story with no plot. What we see in the present – a universe eminently friendly to life forms like ours – is the result of a highly specified history that had to be exactly as it was.

Start with the Big Bang, out of which everything emerged initially. The expansion rate has to be set precisely. Too slow and gravity would have pulled everything back into a black hole. Too fast and all the matter would disperse and there would be nothing but isolated atoms spread throughout a vast and lifeless cosmic darkness. In between these two inhospitable extremes is a precise value where gravity can gather atoms into stars but cannot gather all the matter into one big mass.

Stars play a surprisingly important role in making the universe habitable. In the early universe, the only element that exists in any quantity is hydrogen. Gravity gathers these hydrogen atoms into big balls called stars, which are the birthplaces of the rest of the atoms. Most of the heavier elements in the universe – the oxygen and carbon so essential for life – were created in stars through the process of fusion, which is also the process that provides the energy by which stars shine.

Here is how it works. Stars are made mainly of hydrogen but, because the gravity of the star is so great, the hydrogen atoms are compressed so tightly together that they fuse into helium, the second lightest atom. The helium, most of which was formed soon after the Big Bang, fuses with other hydrogen to create lithium, the third lightest atom. Two helium atoms can fuse to create beryllium, the fourth lightest atom. And so on down the periodic table, as a variety of increasingly complex fusion reactions create heavier elements through more fusion.

Some steps on the fusion ladder are improbable. In particular the process that leads to carbon is very curious and seems highly improbable. The details of how this works would take us down a long road so we will not include them here. But it is worth noting that carbon is absolutely critical to life and almost all scientists agree that a universe without carbon would have no life in it.

If you change any of the knobs on your UCM, you will lose the capacity to make carbon, and you'll have a universe with no life in it. In the 1950s, Polkinghorne's colleague, the Cambridge University astronomer Fred Hoyle recognized the precision of this and made this observation: "A commonsense interpretation of the facts suggests that a super-intellect has monkeyed with physics, as well as with chemistry and biology, and that there are no blind forces worth speaking about in nature. The numbers one calculates from the facts seem to me so overwhelming as to put this conclusion almost beyond question."[1]

Hoyle did not suggest that God was the "super-intellect". He was an atheist. The scientific explanation of how carbon formed in stars was well understood. But this explanation provided no insight into how the knobs of the universe got set to precisely those values that would collaborate so remarkably to produce carbon. Hoyle's remark, coming as it does from an atheist, acknowledges just how startling it is that the universe has the exact properties that enable the existence of life.

To get any universe friendly to life out of your UCM, you have to set the knobs extremely close to those values that they have in our universe. But what do we mean by "exactly"? Well, it turns out that if you turn the gravity knob and change gravity by even a tiny fraction of a percent – enough so that you would be, say, one billionth of a gram heavier or lighter when you get on the bathroom scale – the universe becomes so different that there are no stars, galaxies, or planets. No planets – no life.

We need stars to do more than just make carbon and other elements for us. The energy that sustains our planet comes from a star. The sun (one of the stars) has been a steady and stable source of energy for our planet, creating the right atmosphere for life to develop over the past few billion years. The balance of gravity, electromagnetism, and the nuclear forces has made the sun burn in a uniform manner for billions of years. If that balance is disturbed by changing the settings on your UCM, then stars burn too cool to provide adequate energy, or they burn too hot and fast to provide the energy needed for life.

The forces of nature must also collaborate so that some stars can explode at the end of their lives. Otherwise, the elements necessary for life will remain in the cooling corpse of the dead star. Our solar system formed from the debris of just such an exploded star. Every atom in our bodies comes from the ashes of burned-out stars that exploded. Turn the knobs just a bit and stars don't explode at the end of their lives.[2]

The thought experiments conducted on the UCM were quite revealing. All the knobs on your UCM had to be set just right. Adjust any of them, and the universe, like Robert Frost's celebrated traveler, moves through cosmic history along a different path – a path to a universe without life in it. Our universe is friendly to life, but only because the past 14 billion years have unfolded in a particular way that led to the formation of a habitable planet with liquid water and rich chemistry. The early universe did not look very promising, as Polkinghorne notes: "If we peer back fourteen billion years to within a minute fraction of a second of the primal event of the big bang, we have good reason to suppose that there was then a time when the whole universe was a highly energetic soup of quarks and gluons and other exotic particles."[3]

Our universe is a collection of material condensed by gravity, formed through processes that created galaxies, stars, planets, molecules, atoms, and nuclei. The universe is made of material held together by nuclear and electromagnetic forces that result in the existence of simple atoms and complex human beings. The universe looks like it was made for life and scientists have strained to find homey metaphors to help lay people appreciate just how remarkable this is.

Tony Hewish, a Nobel Prize-winning astronomer, says the accuracy of just one of the forces – the setting on its UCM knob – is comparable to getting the mix of flour and sugar right to within one grain of sugar in a cake ten times the mass of the sun.[4] Or it's the equivalent of getting a hole in one in golf when the distance between the tee and the hole is thirteen times the distance between Earth and Pluto.[5]

Fred Hoyle, who we saw above, called the universe a "put-up job". Freeman Dyson, another great scientist who had the soul of a poet put it like this in his biography *Disturbing the Universe*: "The more I examine the universe and the details of its architecture, the more evidence I find that the universe in some sense must have known we were coming."[6] Agnostics, skeptics, deists, and orthodox Christians have all looked at this state of affairs and concluded that there is "Something Else" going on, in addition to what science has discovered.

It's possible, of course, that the Something Else is just

an accident. One speculation is that there really is an actual UCM out there and it has created trillions of other universes and continues to do so, like a magical popcorn maker that can't be turned off. Countless other universes have been started in similar fashion to ours, but because their settings were different from the one we're in, they never became friendly to life. This is the so-called "multi-verse" explanation for the remarkable fine-tuning of our universe.

Polkinghorne is skeptical that the multi-verse explanation actually explains anything. He likes to quote the philosopher John Leslie, who tells the following parable.

Imagine that you are about to be executed by firing squad. You are marched to the execution area, tied to a stake, and see ten expert marksmen raise their guns and aim them at you. The leader yells "Fire!" and you hear the shots. Then something dawns on you. Nothing hurts – you're still here – you survived!

Naturally you would wonder exactly how that happened. Few of us would walk away, shrug our shoulders, and say, "Well, *that* was a close one!" Most of us would want an explanation. Leslie offers two possible explanations. First, there were so many other executions that day, and marksmen can't hit their targets *every single time*, so it was just a mathematical fluke, highly unlikely, quite unbelievable, but within the laws of probability. Fate was on your side, so good for you. Second, the marksmen *intended* to miss. They, not fate – whatever that is – were on your side.[7]

This, says Polkinghorne, is a way to look at why life is possible in this universe and why we are here. It's not satisfying to simply say, "Well, we're here," and leave it at that. It's possible that there are many universes out there with different physical laws and circumstances, and that this is the one out of millions where the knobs were set so precisely – randomly, of course, since it is all done by "fate" – that allowed for carbon-based life.

It's also possible that this is the only universe there is, and that it was created in such a way that it allowed for the fruitful kind of life we enjoy.[8] We can choose which explanation seems more satisfactory.

Polkinghorne, and many other scientists, choose the latter explanation. Those who look at the universe as fine-tuned, just-right for life, call this condition the Anthropic Principle, which means that all forces of the universe have combined to make it possible for us to live in it. Still, when we consider the vastness of the universe, it is easy to feel lost in it.

> *When we think of our universe with its trillions*
> *upon trillions of stars, we can easily get upset about*
> *our apparent insignificance as inhabitants of what*
> *is, effectively, just a speck of cosmic dust. We should*
> *not, though, because if all those stars were not there,*
> *we wouldn't be here to be daunted by the thought of*
> *them… Only a cosmos at least as big as ours could*
> *endure for the fourteen billion years necessary for*
> *evolving carbon-based life. You need ten billion*
> *years for the first generation stars to make the*
> *carbon, then about four billion years for evolution*
> *to yield beings of our sort of complexity. It's a process*
> *that just can't be hurried.*[9]

Nor can it be attributed to good luck. "It is a remarkable fact that the world was created for life," he said. "It's absurdly irrational to think it's good luck. Were there trillions of experiments to get this fine tuning? That's highly speculative. It's a metaphysical guess either way. There are an infinite number of even integers, but none of them has the property of oddness." This is an important analogy. Just because you have a UCM that produced an infinity of universes does not mean you will produce all possible universes. A machine that generated an infinity of numbers might never produce an even number, or an irrational number like pi. The machine would have to be "tuned" itself in some way to guarantee that it covered the relevant possibilities.

Polkinghorne had no "Aha!" moment when he realized that the world was fine-tuned for life, but his study of physics led him there. "It's natural for a scientist to search for understanding and to make sense of aspects of the world," he said. "You become more dissatisfied with partial understanding. Science encourages this."

He began considering the Anthropic Principle when academic papers were first published on it in the 1960s. All scientists, he said, were interested in the topic. "Before, the view was that our universe was unremarkable, so this was very interesting," he said. As a person of faith, Polkinghorne saw the significance of scientists concluding that the universe was just right for life to occur. "It wasn't a knock-down proof, but it was an important part of the case," he said. "I already believed the world was God's creation. I just didn't realize God had to be so careful."

All of these particulars working in the just-right way for life to occur motivate Polkinghorne to believe that there is a Mind involved.

> *My instinct, as a scientist, is to try to understand things as thoroughly as possible. I can't give up a lifetime's habit just at this point... What I've been saying is that the universe, in its rational beauty and transparency, looks like a world shot through with signs of mind, and, maybe, it's a capital M Mind of God we are seeing. In other words, the reason within and the reason without fit together because they have a common origin in the reason of the Creator, who is the ground of all that is. An ancient verse in Genesis comes to mind, which says*

> *that humanity is made 'in the image of God.' I*
> *actually think this is what makes science possible.*

This is where Polkinghorne insists – adamantly, in fact – that the fine-tuning of the universe does not prove or disprove the existence of God. "I *am* saying that the existence of the Creator would explain why the world is so profoundly intelligible, and I can't see any other explanation that works half as well."[10] No single argument is going to prove or disprove God's existence, of course, but "our power to understand the physical world is just one part of a total case for religious belief," he said.[11]

So the universe is fine-tuned to accommodate life. But does that world make sense to John Polkinghorne? "Yes, but there are puzzles," he said. "It's very superficial to see all things as tested and understood. And to say things just happened to work out for *this* universe is a lazy statement. You have to say that either there is a Divine Mind or that we hold the winning lottery ticket."

Not everyone buys into the significance of the Anthropic Principle, though. Stephen Hawking puts it like this: "The human race is just a chemical scum on a moderate-sized planet."[12] Polkinghorne shakes his head at statements like this. "It's *reductio ad absurdum*," he said. "That's like the argument that music is only the vibration of horse hair across tightened strings in a wooden structure. People make extreme statements in studies that don't correspond at all to real life."

For Polkinghorne, the evidence that conditions were made "just right" for life is enough for him to believe God made it all for a purpose. "Asking and answering the questions, 'Why can we do science at all?' and 'Why is the universe so special?' have given us a nudge in the direction of religious belief," he said. "The answers we've found do suggest that there's Someone there. I've already agreed that it doesn't amount to proof, but I think there aren't many really important things that can be established in this kind of purely logical and necessary way." He cites scientists like Hoyle and Paul Davies, neither of whom declares allegiance to any religious beliefs, who also believe that the beauty and balance of the world implies that there is some kind of mind behind it. "It may seem bizarre," Davies said, "but in my opinion science offers a surer path to God than religion."[13]

In the 14 billion years from the Big Bang to the present, a lot has happened. But it doesn't really appear, especially if you stand back to get perspective, that it was all just randomness. Polkinghorne, with the intuitions of a physicist and the eye of a believer, sees this cosmic story as full of purpose.

"A universe that, when it was a ten thousand millionth of a second old, was just a hot soup of elementary particles has become the home of saints and scientists. Remember, this has only been possible because the universe has anthropic fine-tuning built into its physical fabric. Such astonishing fertility doesn't look like a purposeless world of accident."[14] Where those particles came from in the first place is something we will probably never know, Polkinghorne said. "It's not accessible to us. We can only see the aftermath of the Big Bang. We can't think of the universe in a coherent way at the very beginning."

Holmes Rolston, the grand old man of environmentalism, has a homey analogy. He notes that when an astronomer gazes through a telescope at some far-away galaxy, the most complex physical structure known to man is just six inches away from the eyepiece that is looking into the stars. It is inside the skull of the astronomer. The ball of energy from 14 billion years ago eventually created our brains. "This recognition in itself might raise the question of whether there has not been more going on in cosmic history than science alone can fully express," Polkinghorne said. "Might there not be some purpose behind it all?"[15] Life did not appear for 10 billion years after the Big Bang, and self-conscious life didn't appear until about 14 billion years, but all of the raw material necessary for both was present in that initial moment. "Its physical fabric was then of the exact form necessary to allow the eventual emergence of life," he said.[16]

Science tells us that we live in a universe whose rational beauty makes it seem like a mind was involved from the beginning, and that the possibility of carbon-based life was present at this beginning. But science can't tell us any more than that. "Yet, if we are people endowed with a thirst for the kind of intellectual satisfaction that comes from gaining understanding through and through, it does not seem sufficient just to treat these remarkable properties as happy accidents. They surely signal the need for a deeper form of intelligibility, going beyond the scientific."[17]

The demand for that deeper intelligibility motivates Polkinghorne toward believing in God. "The world that science describes seems to me, with its order, intelligibility, potentiality and tightly-knit character, to be one that is consonant with the idea that it is the expression of the will of a Creator, subtle, patient and content to achieve his purposes by the slow unfolding of process inherent in those laws of nature which, in their regularity, are but the pale reflections of his abiding faithfulness."[18]

But if the universe was created for life as we understand it, what is the purpose of that life? "The meaning of the universe is that it is endowed by God to allow creatures to arise – some who will know their creator – into a closer relationship between creature and creator." The universe is God's project to create creatures to love and be loved, where God can love, and where the creation can love God. Another way to think about it is to say that the *purpose* of the world is to experience what it is becoming.

Polkinghorne sees his individual purpose as "living a faithful Christian life, with some compassionate concern for others who cross my path. I want to be faithful in worship and prayer, and be a faithful witness of the Truth in my writing and speaking." And while he may still wonder from time to time if it's all true, "I have never thought the universe was a tale told by an idiot."

One of the ways he understands how the world is still evolving and still creating itself is watching his own children grow. "As a father, the gift of love I gave to my children was the gift of a degree of independence," he said. "Parents know that children have to make themselves. That's how God is with us and how he is with the universe." When one of his children would make a decision that Polkinghorne believed was not in the child's best interest, he showed restraint. "I did not force my own wishes and could not feel disappointed," he said. "God works this way in that he tries to maximize the outcome to bring about divine fulfillment. We see our children become themselves, fulfilling their gifts and talents. The parent analogy is imperfect, but it is a way of seeing the point."

The dynamics at play in this universe combine to give us freedom to participate in the unfolding process of a universe that is still being created. This could not happen in just "any old world," Polkinghorne states. "That the universe is capable of such fruitfulness speaks to me of a divine purpose expressed in the given structure of the world," he said.[19]

This does not imply that the purpose of creation was to produce Homo sapiens, he said. "If God is creator, then all creatures matter to God, appropriate to their nature. Colossians 1 speaks about *all* things. In Job, God speaks out of the whirlwind and says, 'Look at the hippopotamus. I made him as I made you."

Discussions of God's purpose and activity in the world often evolve into a simplistic theology with an overly personal God who helps us find parking places in shopping malls and protects us from car accidents while other passengers are inexplicably injured or killed. And, while this may be too simplistic, the God of Christianity is active in the world, doing things that seem purposeful and reasonable. Both the Anthropic Principle and the Bible seem to imply that God is a personal God. As creator of the universe, he made it just right for life. He also led Israel out of Egypt and raised Jesus from the dead. "However obscure their modality, these events involve acts of God, or Christianity is profoundly in error," Polkinghorne said. "The paradoxes of providence are not mere intellectual puzzles. They arise from the heart of religious experience."[20] The rationality of Christian theology derives from its ability to make sense of God's actions in the world.

But what are God's motives for this creation that began with the Big Bang and continues to be created? Is there a reason adequate to explain such a grand project? God created the world, says Polkinghorne, "To have freely acting beings who could experience love. God's nature of love is fulfilled in the act of creation of creaturely others to live in relationship with him." Polkinghorne views creation as more than the result we can see and experience now. It is a continuous, progressive unfolding of the world. Mountains erode and others are thrust upward. Land masses shift. The landscape is in continual flux. Creation is ongoing – evolving. Creation is in the ongoing process of making itself. "God shares the unfolding course of creation with creatures, who have their divinely allowed, but not divinely dictated, roles to play in its fruitful becoming," he said. "It was an act of divine generosity that enables others to be. He is not incomplete without creation."[21]

But since it has been allowed some freedom to make itself, the world has painful side effects. "Creatures will behave in accordance with their natures: lions will kill their prey; earthquakes will happen; volcanoes will erupt and rivers flood."[22] God will interact with all levels of this creation as it creates itself, but will not overrule it. He won't keep the murderer from killing, or the earthquake from destroying. He won't shut gravity off temporarily just because a toddler falls out a window. God will allow space for all creatures to act, including gravity.[23] On a microscopic level, cells are allowed to mutate and turn into cancer. "Lots of things happen that don't have a purpose. The three great periods of extinction, for instance. But even they were always followed by an exuberance of life. Why do people become ill? It is unsatisfying to say they were crushed by the juggernaut of evolution. When we see how the world works we see that genetic mutation induces new forms of life *and* malignancy. That may be true, but it's not the whole truth."

How God interacts with the creation is also subject to change as that creation evolves. God related differently to the universe in the moments after the Big Bang, when it was a ball of energy, than with a world containing human beings. And he will relate differently millions of years from now as creation continues to create. "As Christians we feel special because the Word came and lived among us. In the history of the world, there is astonishing and unexpected emergence of new things, such as life giving rise to self-consciousness. There could be more that is unrealized. It's not clear whether future generations will be superior."

For now, though, it is a relationship that allows for independence, the way loving parents allow their children to become their true selves. Charles Kingsley said that the Creator could no doubt have brought into being a world ready made, but instead did something even more unusual – he allowed for a creation to make itself.[24] And as parents can't know for sure how their children are going to turn out, Polkinghorne says that a similar dynamic exists for God and creation. "Even he does not know the unformed future, and that is no imperfection in the divine nature, for that future is not yet there to be known."[25] It's an unfolding improvisation, and not the performance of an already written score.[26]

Ultimately, Polkinghorne believes, the universe and the ability to explore its beauty are part of the Father's gift. "The beautiful rational order of the universe is the imprint of the divine Logos, 'without whom was not anything made that was made' (John 1:3). Whether acknowledged or not, it is the Holy Spirit, the Spirit of truth (John 15:26), who is at work in the truth-seeking community of scientists. That community's repeated experiences of wonder at the disclosed order of the universe are, in fact, tacit acts of the worship of its Creator."[27] Our ability to observe the universe gives us a glimpse into the veiled presence of the Divine Mind, which leads Polkinghorne into a state of worship and hope for an eternal purpose beyond this world.

When Bach's Mass in B Minor concludes, there is outward silence. To the listener, though, the notes resonate, and still sound just right.

CHAPTER SIX
Law and Order

The couple arriving at the house are happy to see John Polkinghorne, welcoming and framed in the doorway. There are handshakes and embraces. The umbrella is stowed in the corner – a light afternoon rain had been falling. There is small talk while the ubiquitous English tea is prepared: Yes, the traffic was particularly bad this morning; yes that rain last night really soaked the town; yes, the prime minister really went out on a limb with that last decision. The tea is poured and they settle in the sitting room; the couple present Polkinghorne with their dilemma – the real reason for their visit.

Years earlier their young adult daughter had a serious surgical procedure. Because the surgery would make it impossible for her to bear children, the family had some of her eggs removed in case she might one day want to find a surrogate mother to carry her biological children. The daughter was older and healthy now, and wanted to have someone carry a baby for her.

But there was a problem. The eggs were removed from the daughter almost six years prior. British law required that eggs be destroyed after being frozen for six years, because of fears that the long-term freezing would compromise the eggs. It was an old law, and new research had shown that long-term freezing does not reduce the viability of the eggs. The old law was still on the books and still being enforced. By the time the family could find a surrogate mother for the eggs, they would be past their legal time.

The couple was naturally worried about their potential

grandchild falling victim to an obsolete British law. They wondered if Polkinghorne could help: Is there something you can do to create an exception to the law, they pleaded, or, better yet, have the law changed? This is not the kind of question, of course, couples typically ask of their priests or physics professors.

"I told them that I probably didn't have the kind of influence in government that they thought I had," he said. "I said their best bet was to find a journalist who could tell their story and through public pressure, grant the eggs a reprieve."

Still, he wrote a letter on the couple's behalf to the national lawmakers, recommending they allow this exception, and that they consider redrafting legislation based on new science. It was the "right" thing to do, which meant that Polkinghorne would do it.

In the midst of life's dilemmas people are often called upon to "do what is right". Undergirding such experiences is the assumption that we can somehow know what is "the right thing". But where does that sense come from? Knowing there is a right and wrong carries the implication that there is a vast matrix of morality that drives our behavior. Every playground in the world hears "It's not fair!" chanted by the children playing on them. We are constantly summoned to fairness on everything from tax rates to the purchase of imported coffee.

Polkinghorne has lived his entire life with an acute sense that there is a reality to the concept of fairness. He remembers playing at a neighbor's house with a childhood friend. They were in the kitchen fooling around with an old-fashioned manual clothes-wringing apparatus, and John unscrewed the handle, causing it to fall off. Convinced he had broken it, he ran back to his house to the familiar security of his own room, where he waited, full of dread. Eventually his mother arrived and asked him what was wrong. He told her what he had done, and they went back to the neighbor's house and fixed the handle. "My concept of right and wrong is as early as my conscious memory," he said.

Childhood issues of fairness were common and, like children have always done, John often protested when things seemed unfair. "When I was little our neighbor left a cricket bat by our front door for my brother and me to play with," he said, recalling one such occasion. "But Peter and I argued about whose it was. Our neighbor must have heard that argument, because the next day there was another cricket bat by our door!"

As he grew older Polkinghorne's insight into issues of ethics and morality became sophisticated and acute. He became known for his ability to navigate complex ethical waterways with boldness and clarity, the very reason why the couple had come to call on him. John was widely known by this time for his work with groups throughout England that were dealing with medical ethics. He chaired a committee that oversaw the code of practice for fetal tissue research that, at the time, was targeted at Parkinson's disease. Other committee members included the president of the Royal College of Physicians, a national expert on medical law and ethics, and a medical sociologist. Polkinghorne also chaired a national review board that dealt with policies related to substance abuse.

His most prominent work on high-profile national committees was as a member of the Human Genetics Commission, which evaluated the ethical consequences of recent advances in human genetic research. He chaired the committee on genetic testing, developing guidelines to prevent people from being subjected to genetic testing without their knowledge, and to develop regulations on the use of genetic information. The committee listened to presentations by experts and discussed what should be done with this rapidly growing knowledge and frightening technology. Polkinghorne, who had spent years teaching the most advanced mathematical physics to some of the greatest minds of his generation, was the consummate teacher on these committees.

He could fuse the science with the philosophy in a way that often moved everyone toward consensus. Scientists, often eager to push recklessly ahead with their research learned the value of moral reflection and dialogue; non-scientists, nervous that science was blindly inaugurating a "brave new world" came to understand the great promise of research and the many benefits likely to ensue from it. He had come a long way from the little boy who quarreled over the fairness of his brother getting the mysterious cricket bat that appeared at their door.

Polkinghorne also helped develop the policy regarding research on stem cells and embryos. These rules, still in effect, specify, on a case-by-case basis, whether research is allowed on embryos no older than fourteen days. This emotionally charged area demands great wisdom as there are still many people who think of such early stage embryos as "tiny people" when, in fact, even at fourteen days they are still without the beginning of a central nervous system and thus unable to engage in any "human" interaction with the world. A fourteen-day old embryo, says Polkinghorne, is "an undifferentiated mass of totipotent stem cells."[1]

"The issue with embryonic testing is that human beings are ends, not means, not to be treated for anything but for their own benefit," he said. Whether one can do embryonic testing at all depends on one's view of human nature. "It's quite natural to say life begins at conception, that it's a person at that point, or you could take a developmental view that says a person is something you grow into." The great medieval theologian, Thomas Aquinas agreed with Aristotle, the scientific authority of his day, who said that it took forty days for a male embryo to become a person, and eighty days for a female. These details are not rooted in careful scientific research, of course, but Aquinas's position was important because it showed that the Christian tradition has not historically treated newly fertilized eggs as fully human.

Polkinghorne was greatly relieved to reach an agreement

about the fourteen-day rule, because there was a serious sub-text to the discussion. "One of the difficult aspects was to decide which were the questions we *had* to answer, and which ones were not," he said. "The cell tissue we were discussing had to come from abortions. But we didn't have to answer the abortion question. That's a different discussion."

Polkinghorne enjoyed the important work done by these committees, but he also enjoyed the way in which the work was accomplished. "They were collections of people trying to find a common mind, finding a right way ahead, not trying to win an argument," he said. As opposed to the polarized stalemate that exists in much public discussion, these groups sought constructive dialogue. They knew there was value in hearing each other out. "I lament that we don't seem to have many meeting places these days to have temperate discussions on important issues," he said.

Polkinghorne is gifted at creating an atmosphere where other views can be heard. In the late 1990s he was invited by the German theologian Michael Welker to participate in discussions with a group of scholars at the Center of Theological Inquiry at Princeton. Jürgen Moltmann was there, as was Miroslav Volf, a famous theologian from Croatia. They gathered in an ornate, paneled room for three days at a time, twice a year for three years. Each would give a short paper and lead a discussion on provocative and esoteric topics. They discussed divine action and the nature of the "end times". The meetings led to books such as *The End of the World and the Ends of God*, edited by Polkinghorne and Welker, and Polkinghorne's own book, *The God of Hope and The End of the World*. A paper he wrote for the group on God's relationship to time became a chapter in his book *Faith, Science and Understanding*.

He loved the experience. "There were very diverse opinions in that group and it was mentally stimulating," he said. "Exhilarating, actually."

For the Church of England, Polkinghorne was part of the

fifteen-member Doctrine Commission, which included N. T. Wright, then bishop of Durham and considered by many to be the world's leading New Testament scholar. As a group they wrote books on the Holy Spirit, salvation, and other topics. The spirited discussions were often quite animated, but they would eventually arrive at a consensus. "Because of the diversity of the group and the breadth of the topics, I thought during the first year that it would never work," he said. "By the second year we saw a convergence. Group activity is important to me, and this was an extraordinarily enjoyable one." Polkinghorne was also part of the Church of England's General Synod during that critical period when it debated and then approved the ordination of women to the priesthood.

Polkinghorne's contributions to medical ethics and genetic testing were of such nationally recognized significance that in 1997 he was knighted by Queen Elizabeth. Technically one cannot call him Sir John, though, despite the recognition. In Britain there is an ancient custom prohibiting calling knighted Anglican priests "Sir". "I am inclined to suppose it to have something to do with the fact that we are not allowed to stick swords into people, though in the Middle Ages the clergy were permitted to hit people on the head with a heavy mace, provided they did not draw blood," he said.[2]

Newly created knights are asked what symbols they want on their personal coat of arms. Polkinghorne chose three: a lion because that is on the coat of arms of Trinity College; an h-slash, symbolizing Planck's Constant, named after Max Planck, one of the founders of quantum theory; and a pelican, the symbol of the Perse School, which he attended as a boy in Cambridge. The knighting ceremony was formal, as one would expect of an occasion embodying so much British history. The video account, however, shows Polkinghorne in casual and light-hearted conversation with the queen. The affable priest who once knocked on the doors of strangers in Blean and who engaged the greatest physicists of the twentieth century was not intimidated by the queen.

"She asked about my ethics work," he said. "It was a moving and proud occasion, and it was nice to share it with my family. There are echoes of history in it. This kind of ceremony is one of the things we're good at in this country."

As a theologically informed scientist with the heart of a village priest, Polkinghorne's insights into the ethics of research are profound and singular. He knows that science helps us find truth, and that improves our lives. It gives us knowledge, which is presumably more desirable than ignorance. He also knows that science, and its "lusty offspring" technology, can improve our lives in ways we could not have imagined just a few years ago. But this science-bred technology comes with unintended consequences that often involve ethical complications. Those complications have convinced Polkinghorne that "not everything that can be done should be done."[3] Advances in technology are not typically accompanied by advances in wisdom and discernment. There is a danger for a researcher buoyed up by the excitement of discovery to be carried away, seduced by the siren call of knowledge. "The world is the gift of the divine Creator, not the construct of a human exploiter," he said.[4] All of society – not just the researchers holding kites in the lightning storm – must be part of the discussion as to whether one can do embryonic manipulation. A broad conversation is needed to decide where it will go, how it will get there, and why it will go at all, he said. Perhaps no subject illustrates this need for broad discussion as the subject of genetics research. "Law and morality do not necessarily coincide," he said.[5]

In his work on the national agenda for embryonic stem cell research, he wrestled with the position of the Roman Catholic Church that considers an embryo to be a full human person from the moment of conception. From that perspective, harvesting embryonic stem cells for therapeutic uses would be ethically unacceptable. The necessary destruction of the embryo would be the murder of a human life. Polkinghorne recognizes the Catholic concern but thinks it goes too far.

"The very early embryo is entitled to a deep moral respect because of its potential personhood, so that it is not just a speck of protoplasm that you can do what you like with and then flush it down the sink when you have finished with it, but it is not yet a full human being," he said. "One might say that it has a human life, but it has not yet attained human personhood."[6]

In his own family, these biotechnological concerns assumed center stage when Polkinghorne's granddaughter was born with Down syndrome, at the very time the grandfather was deep into his work on the national bioethics committee. Many consider a Down syndrome pregnancy so tragic they choose to abort, if they know in time. But Polkinghorne's family was content that they had not known ahead of time, since they would not have considered an abortion. "Having a Down syndrome baby made us more aware of the need to support and care for my daughter and granddaughter," Polkinghorne said. "But Down syndrome is not like many handicaps, like Huntington's disease, which if we could eliminate, that would be a good thing. My daughter declined having an amniocentesis for her next child because she knew she wouldn't have an abortion, so why know? We know that the world can be strange and bitter. But this experience did not alter my views on embryo research." In fact, the arrival of this granddaughter shattered whatever images Polkinghorne had about Down syndrome children. "Knowing her liberates you from those stereotypes of a handicapped person," he said. "There's a simplicity to her that is wonderful. I can't conceive of her not being a member of our family."

Technological breakthroughs have a long history of creating ethical challenges and nowhere is this more dramatic than in reproduction. From birth control pills opening a door to promiscuity, to ultrasounds providing information that leads many women to abort there is a long history of challenging linkages between technology and the ethics of sex and reproduction. Such conversations, as we know from the daily headlines, are incredibly polarizing. Loud voices on both sides of ethical questions project a remarkable confidence that they represent the "truth." Often everyone in the debate has a clear sense that the issue is one of "right and wrong" – the disagreement is simply over which side is right and which is wrong. In the background of such debates, however, a deep question lurks. Where do we get that sense of right and wrong? And what compels us to stand up for what is "right," once we have confidence we know what it is? Does the universe itself have a moral dimension? Are there moral laws in the same way that there are scientific laws?

"Of course there are moral laws," Polkinghorne said. "Torturing children is wrong. That's a fact we know as clearly as anything. Truth is better than a lie – with some exceptions. The weak are not to be discarded. Part of the argument for God is that the world is endowed with morality."

Through the long slow process of evolution, humans developed morality and altruism, he said, a view that seems counter to the "survival of the fittest" rule that drives the evolutionary process. Richard Dawkins, for example, has argued that the law of the selfish gene rules evolution. Our genes are wired to preserve and reproduce themselves; genes that are good at this persist and spread; genes that are not gradually die out. Our genes have constructed bodies to house, protect, and reproduce them; these bodies also behave selfishly, and so do our fully grown bodies, according to Dawkins. These genes also motivate us to protect our offspring and close relatives, since they share our genes. And they may even motivate us to care about our "tribe" since the health of our tribe is related to our ability to flourish and reproduce. These behaviors may appear altruistic – fighting off a lion that threatens one's children, for example – but, at the most fundamental level, the altruist is really just protecting other creatures that probably share many genes with their altruistic benefactor. But that's not the whole story, says Polkinghorne. Altruism does protect one's genetic legacy, he said, "but there is an irreducible characteristic about right and wrong. We *know* something is the right thing to do."

Polkinghorne is convinced that the world is much richer than the purely materialistic view that undergirds the worldview of people like Dawkins. Our deep intuitions about right and wrong are not fantasies. When we assure our frightened children that all will be well, "The culture didn't teach us that," he said. "It's innate. So is the knowledge that love is better than hate. In the parable of the sheep and goats that Jesus tells in Matthew 25, the sheep didn't know they were being good. They just were." Some people have risked and even given their lives for total strangers, making the snap decision to do so. We intuitively know that Mother Teresa and Oscar Schindler embody a real, but elusive feature of the world. "Love of that incalculable kind eludes Darwinian explanation," he said.[7]

But, while we may be born with moral imperatives that seem like scientific laws, the comparison ultimately breaks down. "I have no choice in accepting the law of gravity," Polkinghorne notes, "while I have a choice of whether to love my neighbor as myself." Ideally, religion should help us with the moral imperatives. "Yes, religion ought to be helpful, but we don't have an untarnished record of this. Religion can also mislead us. There are many spine-chilling paradoxes of unthinking religious actions. In one of the crusades, a bishop said 'Kill them all – God will know his own.'"

In the Bible, particularly the Old Testament, atrocities were commonly committed in the name of God. "But that's only part of the story," he said. "There is also a lot about caring for slaves, for the immigrants, for the poor. We must recognize the imperfection of religion. It's a process of unveiling. Yes, there is the book of Judges and all of the brutality, where the way to serve God is to exterminate others. That's a crude and insufficient understanding. But eventually we get to Isaiah and Hosea. It only makes sense as a developing story."

In early biblical writings, entire families were punished for one member's sin. Later, responsibility moves from familial to personal, which is more consistent with how we think about this today. In the modern era, despite the insights that have developed over time, we note with shame that it took hundreds of years for religion to see that slavery was wrong. "The foundational issues are there from the beginning, but doctrine develops in a continuously unfolding way," Polkinghorne said. Scripture speaks in language contemporary with its origin. It speaks most clearly to the culture of its time, so we must continually ask what is time-bound and what is everlasting? "Some people say that they take Scripture literally, but absolutely no one takes Scripture literally," argues Polkinghorne. "It's attractive to say we do because the judgment in it is so clear, so black and white. But no one is taking children outside the gates and stoning them. There are shades of grey in all of it."

The contradictory portrayals of God in the Bible, of how authority should be viewed, of how enemies are to be treated, are all "fatal to the theory of using it as a divinely-guaranteed textbook," Polkinghorne warns. "Those who attempt to do so either construct a tacit canon within the canon, omitting what is awkward and unseemly, or they are driven to frustration or crazy ingenuity in trying to reconcile the irreconcilable, to square the God of love with the command to Saul utterly to destroy the Amalekites (1 Samuel 15). If the reading of Scripture is to be truly edifying, it will have to be in some other mode than this."[8] The Bible can't be tied down, he said, but must be viewed as "having multi-layered meaning, capable of mediating many messages to its readers."[9] But those messages must be seen in the totality of the message of the Bible, not in the selective nature that animates the shrill voices. "An à la carte approach, relying on carefully selected favorite passages, would be an unacceptable impoverishment," he said.[10]

A bewildering richness and conflict of life runs through Scripture, but underneath it all is the unifying principle, testifying of God's love through Christ.[11] It isn't a textbook, providing answers to life's difficult questions for us to memorize for some future examination. "Scripture is not an unchallengeable set of propositions demanding unquestioning assent, but it is *evidence*, the record of foundational spiritual experience, the laboratory notebooks of gifted observers of God's ways with men and women."[12] The Bible, despite being routinely bound as a single volume, is not a book, but more of a library.[13] It provides *motivation* for belief.

An evolving understanding of the Scriptures has an important analog in science. Just as science moved past Newton's view of a precise, mechanical, clock-like universe[14] and embraced quantum theory's cloudier, murkier view, religion must also be understood as a developing revelation. "We didn't throw Newton out, but Newton didn't tell the whole story," Polkinghorne said. It's a world with some clocks, and lots of clouds.

If our sense of morality has developed over time as human culture has evolved, then so has our view of God. Our concept of God moves from a thundering voice commanding the destruction of our enemies to the agape love of a gentle Messiah commanding the exact opposite. The earliest biblical documents acknowledge some kind of reality of other gods, as is evident from the wording in the first commandment. But by Isaiah, a few centuries later, there is only one God. But the followers of this one God use this very uniqueness as a justification for killing those who believe in other gods. "This should not be a surprising thought," Polkinghorne said. "We have a developing character. We have an evolving view of God because God is constantly revealing his nature." That doesn't mean, though, that we're evolving away from our need for God, as some philosophers suggest. As we see more of God's love-based nature, we see an even greater need for relationship with God, not an independence. "There has been a clearer understanding of the moral imperative, but has there been progress in fulfilling that imperative in the past century? There may be more insight available, but it's not any easier to follow it. That only shows how much we need God," says Polkinghorne.

One important application of our evolving view of God is in medicine. Biblical accounts of people with certain afflictions are now explained rather differently by science. Legion, the man possessed by demons, would be diagnosed today as a schizophrenic and treated with medicine. Ezekiel had visions and was silent for weeks. "He was probably schizophrenic, too," Polkinghorne said.

In Anne Fadimain's book *The Spirit Catches You and You Fall Down*, a family of immigrants from Laos settles in Fresno, California. The family has a baby who suffers from epilepsy. Child Protective Services and local doctors want to treat the baby and control the seizures, but the family believes this condition is a special gift from God. The rest of the book develops that clash of understandings – modern medicine meets first century Asia. With epilepsy in particular, science can now explain what is happening in the brain and why.

"The fact that there's a biochemical explanation isn't the whole story," Polkinghorne said. "It's like the discussion of music. Is it *just* a matter of endorphins being released in my brain? All this tells us is that we are embodied beings – the spiritual has a scientific counterpart. It's still the *person* having the seizure. The people telling the stories in the Bible were using the language of the day. This just illustrates the psychosomatic unity of a person."

Believing that our understanding of God, right and wrong,

and morality evolves makes those critically important ideas complicated and unclear. That's not what the sound-bite culture of our generation wants. "All ethical discourse is dominated by single issue groups," Polkinghorne laments. "Bioethics in particular raises a level of shrillness, of shouting right or wrong. It would be nice if the Church could put together a dialogue, a forum for drawing people together, instead of making it gladiatorial!"

Polkinghorne finds deep insights into moral laws in many places, including on the bookshelves of his sitting room – in the great works of literature. Physical science may deal with morality and laws on an impersonal level. With literature, it's personal. "One of our principal sources of understanding of what it means to be human is given us through the great literature of the world," he said. "Often it is apparently secular in its character, though I believe that in reality it is based on hidden foundations in the sacredness of life. Literature's deepest insights do not come from tales of a generalized Everyman figure, but from the specificities of an Emma Woodhouse or an Alyosha Karamazov."[15] Polkinghorne said the section in Dostoevsky's *Brothers Karamazov* commonly referred to as "The Grand Inquisitor", is one of the best examples of a story revealing the tensions of human freedom, suffering, and ultimate ambiguity regarding life on earth.

"The Grand Inquisitor is a comparatively concise parable, self-contained," he said. "It has a powerful judgmental image of the church that has sought to exercise power in unChrist-like ways. It's deeply moving. It's an image that sticks with you. Dostoevsky hit the target. In literature, Russian life is more histrionic, uses bolder colors, stands out more. Someone said that Dostoevsky was the wickedest Christian he knew." The Grand Inquisitor parable depicts a wrestling match between good and evil, light and darkness, and gives a twist on the story of Jesus being tempted by Satan.

"My lasting impression of *Brothers Karamazov* is that all Dostoevsky characters take the spiritual life seriously." There are spiritual overtones in Dickens and Austen, too, he said, but not as intense. "In English literature it's more temperate and well-mannered," he said.

The essence of literature is to portray human beings in the human condition. Literature will therefore typically include a degree of morality, he said.

> *I love the creativity of Dickens. You really meet the people of those stories. In* The Pickwick Papers, *when the main character takes a cab and has an altercation with the driver, that cab driver is a real person. His stories are populated by a crowd of real people. With Jane Austen it's a smaller cast in a small middle-class world. She had the extraordinary ability to portray a character through what that person would say. She portrayed a world of real people. Dostoevsky's novels had a smaller crowd where the characters had intense struggles that were shot through with good and evil. Literature portrays the deepest human experience.*

A few months after their visit with Polkinghorne to discuss their daughter's eggs that had been frozen for six years, the couple received a letter from the British government. Their request that the eggs be allowed more time in their cryogenic state was granted, to their great relief. Polkinghorne acknowledges that he wrote a letter on the couple's behalf, but the favor he requested was under discussion and would soon become law. "Still, I guess it helps to be able to sign KBE after your name," he said (KBE stands for Knight Commander of the Order of the British Empire).

CHAPTER SEVEN
Life After Life

John Polkinghorne climbs the stairs in his house, as he has so many times over the years. The stairs are familiar, but the climb grows harder each year. He turns left at the top and enters the spare bedroom at the end of the hallway. Just inside the door is a large black case. He lays it on the carpeted floor and slowly loosens each latch until the lid can be lifted. The open case reveals a light brown cello. The marks on the instrument reveal it was not just a showpiece – it had produced a lot of music over its lifetime. The bow is frayed. It, too, had played many classical pieces in the community orchestras of Cambridge. Polkinghorne gazes at the cello, rests his hand on it briefly, and then closes the lid. He returns the instrument to its place against the wall, in the spare bedroom at the end of the hall.

It took three and a half years for Polkinghorne's wife Ruth to make that cello. She played it lovingly and now it's a family heirloom. One can see it, touch it, recall the low, supportive notes that it once produced, and in doing so, remember a departed loved one. There is, of course, no question as to where Ruth's cello is – it's in the spare bedroom at the end of the hall. Polkinghorne visits the cello there from time to time, as a way to recall those happier times when Ruth played that cello. The visits to the cello are one way that a lonely man can recover something of a happier time when he shared his house with a beloved spouse. But Ruth is not there, in the room at the end of the hall. It is just a place where pleasant memories orbit about a very special cello.

"Where is Ruth now?" Polkinghorne asked, echoing a familiar question that people have asked for millennia. "All I can say is that she's safe with God. When I pray for her it's a formal prayer, for her to rest eternal, rest in peace, and rise in glory. It's not very articulate. I can't be very specific because I don't know her circumstances. But I pray for her as a way to connect."

Polkinghorne has thought carefully about this question for decades and has, as befits a rigorously trained scientist and theologian, a strictly intellectual response to the question: Where is Ruth? Polkinghorne believes that the information pattern of her life is not lost but is preserved, held in the Mind of God.

Human identity is a complex concept. Envisioning eternal continuity of that identity – a central Christian doctrine – is even more complex. Anyone who has buried an elderly parent struck down by a chronic illness has no desire for that phase of their mother or father's life to be extended. How then do we relate our constantly changing earthly identity to the eternal life we affirm as the "resurrection of the body"?

John Polkinghorne, after eight decades of life, is not the same person he was when he was a little boy counting sea shells on the coast of the Bristol Channel. He is not the same person he was at the Quaker elementary school he attended, nor the same person who attended the University of Cambridge, nor who helped explain the existence of the quark, nor who was priest in the village of Blean, nor who occupied the President's Lodge at Queens' College, nor who received membership into the Royal Society, nor who was knighted by the queen, nor who wrote more than thirty books. He's not even the same person he was two years ago. Neither are you. Even the molecules that make up our bodies change about every two years. The chemical make up that was John Polkinghorne in, say, 1950, is completely different from the make up in 2010. Some of his

1950 molecules are probably now a part of other individuals.

So what keeps him as John Polkinghorne, other than his name? What about him has continued? What has carried his "essence" from then to now? Philosophers pose an interesting variation of this question: If a boat is out at sea for a very long time, and it is continuously being repaired while at sea, to a point where every plank has been replaced since it first left the shore, is it still the same boat when it returns? Polkinghorne would say yes, as long as the original pattern of the boat has been maintained. But if drastic changes had taken place, such as the boat leaving the port as a single-hull vessel and returning as a catamaran, then no. "Continuity lies in the pattern and not in the planks," he said.[1]

Similarly human beings are all made of the same molecules – mostly water, many carbon compounds, DNA, and so on. But this does not make them the same person.

Scientists describe a complex "information-bearing pattern" as a way to identify what is unique about each person. This slowly changing pattern represents the core reality of a person and it persists from the beginning of one's life to the end. Memory patterns from childhood, languages learned, profound experiences, all take up residence as neuronal configurations that shape a person through life. Some call this pattern the "soul".

Thomas Aquinas believed that the soul is the form – the information pattern – of the body,[2] and Polkinghorne agrees that this pattern provides the signature of our individual identities. It doesn't consist of atoms and molecules, though, which means it isn't constantly being replaced – only continued. Polkinghorne's view is shared by many contemporary theologians, including his fellow Anglican priest Keith Ward, who was, until 2003, canon of Christ Church, Oxford:

> *The soul is not a little (physical) man sitting inside*
> *the brain. But the human person seems to have a*

dual nature, having both a physically observable body and brain and a rich, colorful, value-laden inner world of experience and thought. These natures are tightly connected, and to separate them would be to leave this world in which we were born and in which we live. Most religious views think we can do this, precisely because the Ultimate Reality is a being or state of pure consciousness, and the goal of religious practice is to achieve union or perfected relationship with that Ultimate Reality.[3]

Polkinghorne says simply, "My soul is the pattern that is me."[4] So if it doesn't consist of complex molecular structures, which would decay upon death, what happens to that pattern that is Ruth or John, or you, at death? Does that pattern continue? Even beyond death? Polkinghorne believes it does.

Christianity has always acknowledged death, especially in the moving accounts of Jesus in Gethsemane and on the cross. "Death is a real end," says Polkinghorne. "However, it need not be an ultimate end, for in Christian understanding only God is ultimate. It is a perfectly coherent hope that the pattern that is a human being could be held in the divine memory after that person's death."[5] The resurrection of Jesus, he says, is the evidence that God at some future point will revitalize those information-bearing patterns of others. In some way, in a form unknown, our lives – our essence – continue after death. The resurrection is the event that inaugurates the new creation,[6] but the world to come will have a different character. It won't be a collection of resuscitated bodies because Jesus' body was not resuscitated. It wasn't just brought back to life after a few days of death. Jesus' resurrection was the sign that a new creation was underway. "The resurrection of Jesus is the seminal event from which the whole of God's new creation has already begun to grow."[7]

Polkinghorne bases his views in part on the argument Jesus had with the Saduccees when they asked him whether there was a destiny beyond death, in Mark 12:18–27. Mentioning Jacob, Isaac, and Abraham, Jesus said, speaking of God: "He is not the God of the dead, but of the living." If the patriarchs mattered to God when they walked the earth, then they still matter to God and they always will. "Their life continues. The same will be true of us. There is no natural hope of a destiny beyond death, a story that science could tell us in terms of its 'horizontal' account of what happens now. But that is not the only story to be told. Religion can tell the 'vertical' story of God's faithfulness, and that story undergirds the hope, already manifested by Jesus' resurrection, that the last word does not lie with death but with God."[8]

We are part of a two-step creative process. "First, the old creation, allowed to explore and realize its potentiality at some metaphysical distance from its Creator; then the redeemed new creation which, through the Cosmic Christ, is brought into a freely embraced and intimate relationship with the life of God."[9]

This view differs from the picture some report when they have near-death experiences, even though these descriptions are strikingly similar to each other. They usually involve a tunnel experience, a greeting by a figure of light, sensations of warmth and welcome, and then an order to return to one's life on earth. Sometimes the experience includes the sense that the person is floating over his or her body. This is usually accompanied by a reluctance to return, but yet a renewed enthusiasm to live the rest of this life to the fullest.[10]

"It is hard to know what to make of these testimonies," he said. "Caution is certainly in order."[11] Are the experiences of light and other similarities the result of a depleting amount of oxygen to the brain? And even though the description differs from Polkinghorne's view of a continuing information-bearing pattern, it still points to something beyond what we know of this life. "I talked to a person who had an experience like this and it so impressed him that it had a lasting effect," he said. "There is something going on there, and there seems to be a consistency of the accounts. But I don't want to make any rash statements."

More wistful accounts often center on a person's fantasy of the perfect life on earth – a fishing trip that extends into eternity, playing golf forever with every shot a hole-in-one, listening to Bach on continuous loop. "If someone has a simplistic view of heaven, as a pastor you can't say, 'Good gracious, it's not that way at all! Your departed husband has better things to do than fishing!' In the life to come we'll be drawing nearer to God. As a priest you're mostly trying to be alongside of people. You can't point out that what they're doing is wishful thinking. What isn't fantasy is the faithfulness of God and the resurrection of Christ. You can only bear witness to what you can speak truthfully. But there is no clinching argument."

In his study as a theologian and a scientist, and in his practice as a vicar, Polkinghorne concedes that nothing can be proven about what happens after death. But he believes there are motivations for hope in a life to come – or to continue – that are reasonable and defensible.

"It seems likely that ever since the Neanderthals began to bury their dead in a fetal position (significant of new birth) and coloured with red ochre (significant of blood and new life), there has been some intuition that death is not the last word in relation to human destiny," he said.[12] One reason people are drawn to speculation about what happens after death is that it helps calibrate the life they are living now. "Ultimately the issue is whether we live in a world that makes sense not just now, but totally and for ever," he said.[13]

We will all die with some things unfulfilled, he said. If it all just disappears when we die, that futility could lead one to believe there is no point to the life they're in right now. "The world makes sense today only if it makes sense everlasting," he said. "That's why it matters what we think about the afterlife."

Thinking of the next life puts *this* life into perspective. "This life is the raw material out of which the new creation comes," he said. Living with the hope of a next world has a direct effect on how we live in this world. "If this is the only life, a life with no hope, then we might as well get as much out of it as we can," he said. "I might want to get out of my unsatisfactory marriage – why not shove off this one and go to another? The temptation would be great. I'll be committed more to this life if I think there is more to life than *just* this life."

There are other reasons for thinking beyond this life. As theology has matured, God's nature has been comprehended with greater clarity as an expression of love. This love is patient and subtle in ways that allow creation and all of its creatures to collaborate with the Creator to make themselves. This deep understanding is consistent with the belief that this expression of love continues beyond death, allowing the ongoing creation to continue. Since creation didn't begin with the snap of divine fingers, why would it end that way?

Our experience offers other hints at a world beyond this one. One of the most provocative comes from mathematics and it is no surprise that mathematicians have rarely been satisfied with a purely materialistic reality. The experience of mathematicians – and Polkinghorne is no exception – is of another dimension "out there". Mathematicians generally interpret their breakthroughs as *discoveries*, rather than *inventions*. Their experience is that of an explorer who finds something that is already there, like a sailor looking for a waterway. Mathematicians speak of "searching" for a solution, never of "inventing" one. Their deep intuition is that the object of their search exists "somewhere" and they will find it if they look hard enough. Prime numbers, to take one example, have always been "there". Their concept and the members of the group have always existed, even before there were people who could do math. And the concept would continue to exist if human beings disappeared. Similarly, the equation describing relativity has always been "there". It took mathematicians and physicists many years to "discover" them. But where had they "been" while waiting to be discovered?

Polkinghorne and others believe there must be another dimension to account for the experience of mathematical discovery. This dimension – for lack of a better term – exists together with the one we know, from which scientists draw these conclusions. Somehow, in ways that seem almost mystical, equations from this "other" reality can be mapped with great detail onto the material features of this reality. There exists an amazing equation that describes the distribution of electrons around the nucleus. A scientist named Erwin Schrödinger discovered it almost a century ago. Newton discovered an amazing equation for gravity three centuries ago. Pythagoras discovered his famous theorem about triangles twenty-five centuries ago.

Thoughtful philosophers have wondered about the reality of this "other" world for as long as philosophers have been able to wonder. So many aspects of our experience point beyond a simple physical reality to a transcendent world. In addition to mathematics, beauty and goodness are hard to explain as manifestation of a purely material reality. How, for example, does one start with protons and electrons, and build a reality that includes great art, literature, and music? Does the reality of such undeniable parts of experience not hint at a greater reality, pointing to something transcendent, outside our traditional views of space and time? "If there are elements of reality beyond the flux of time, then there might also be a destiny beyond the temporal ending of this world," Polkinghorne said.[14]

In his book *A Rumor of Angels*, sociologist Peter Berger

suggests that everyday occurrences naturally point us beyond our temporal existence. When a child has a bad dream and wakes up frightened, to take the example from a previous chapter, the child's parent goes to provide comfort, and often says something like, "It's all right," or "It's going to be okay." When parents offer such comfort to children, are they perpetuating a fantasy about a world where things are not all right and not going to be okay? After all, the world frightening the child includes bullies and dark places, torture and cancer, and concentration camps. Is it possible that parents have tapped into something deeper, more ultimate, where he or she knows that everything really is going to be okay? Polkinghorne is motivated to believe the latter, although he certainly does not construe these hints as proofs.

When one *doesn't* look past the present moment, we see a world that looks amazingly like our present world. "A world obsessed by the present will have only cold memories of the past and apocalyptic fears for the future," he said. "It will be a world of multiple opinions and no shared stories, the setting for a skimpy and etiolated human existence which is a kind of life on half pay."[15] "This life is too hurtful and incomplete to be the whole story."[16]

But what can it mean to affirm that there is more than just this life? Is there anything that can be said about the reality beyond this one? What is in the life to come? Is it more of the same?

It is in addressing these questions that Polkinghorne celebrates the central Christian hope. The world to come will have a different character with a new and intimate way of living with God. "This world is one that contains the focused and covenanted occasions of divine presence that we call sacraments. The new creation will be wholly sacramental, suffused with the presence of the life of God."[17] What we experience in this creation will be transformed and redeemed in a new creation.

The resurrection of Jesus is the model by which we can expect this, Polkinghorne said. "Good Friday was not a charade or an irrelevancy for Jesus. It was an intense and dark experience, plumbing the depths of desolation. But Easter was equally real – not wiping out Good Friday as if it had never happened, but showing that *through death* new life is given by God."[18]

And who, or what, will make up this new creation? Polkinghorne believes it won't just be humans. "This is all speculative, of course, but I can't imagine a new creation devoid of animals," he said. "Humanity is not the only thing God cares about. It's important to see that God is the creator of the whole world, and the whole world is not just a backdrop of the human drama."

So death, consistent with most of Polkinghorne's views, is not the whole story. As humans we are aware of death because we have evolved into self-aware creatures. The Garden of Eden accounts in Genesis show through story what occurred over millions of years. Before Eden, death existed, of course. Entire species, including the dinosaurs, became extinct. But, as humans became aware of themselves and aware of God, death took on an additional dimension. Awareness of death caused mourning and emotional pain.

"Self-conscious beings could anticipate their future death, but at the same time they had become divorced from the God who is the only ground for hope of a destiny beyond that death. Thus humanity became prey to that sadness and frustration at the thought of human transience that we may call mortality. In that sense 'death' – the bitterness of mortality – had truly come into the world and passed to all."[19]

Polkinghorne believes that the emotional pain associated with death is also related to the belief that the spiritual state of the person at death determines how that person will spend eternity.

> *Just as the appeal to continuity based on divine*
> *consistency has led us to expect that the life of*
> *the world to come will be characterized by God's*
> *working through unfolding redemptive process*
> *rather than through instantaneous magic, so we may*
> *also project into that world the love and mercy that*
> *God displays to us in this life. One cannot suppose*
> *that an iron curtain comes down at death and God*
> *says to those caught on the wrong side of it, 'You*
> *had your chance for seventy or eighty years and now*
> *it's too late. No more mercy or forgiveness!' Surely*
> *the God of everlasting love is always ready, like*
> *the father in Jesus' parable, to meet the returning*
> *prodigal whenever he comes to himself and returns*
> *to his true home.*[20]

According to Polkinghorne, that prodigal will have eternity to make that decision.

Polkinghorne is quick to say that this should not imply that how we live and what decisions we make are trivial and insignificant. When Jesus prays "on earth as it is in heaven," he is clearly giving us direction in that our lives should participate in the bringing of heaven to earth. "There is a connection between the two. I want to see realized eschatology, but I don't want it to be *only* that. It's half the experience." Life apart from God now will make it difficult to turn to God in the next life. Divine judgment is actually ultimate self-exposure – divine light – where we are revealed for whoever we really are. "Properly conceived, judgment is the divine antidote to human sin, just as resurrection is the divine antidote to human mortality."[21] But the mercy of God will be present, just as it will be for those who never had the opportunity to learn of God in this life. They "will not be denied that opportunity in the clearer light of the divine presence in the world of the new creation."[22] Much of Jesus' references to hell describe it as Gehenna, the dump outside the city's gates, where fires burn continuously and people cry out in misery. It was a real place, not an imaginary location in eternity, and Jesus' audience knew exactly what he was talking about.

"I don't believe God's offer of love and mercy is withdrawn at death. We still have a free will after death. We're still human beings. That doesn't mean it doesn't matter what we do on earth, but Gehenna is over-interpreted."

Some, though, will simply not know what to do with the opportunity to turn toward God. Polkinghorne's thinking on this is shaped in part by C. S. Lewis's book *The Great Divorce*. This classic Lewis work tells the story of people who get on a bus and leave their drab, grey eternity that is hell (no flames or demons with pitchforks – definitely not Gehenna), to visit heaven through a crack in heaven's floor. In heaven they confront the reality of becoming more and more into the Light that is God. Some can't stand that prospect, though, because it means they won't be able to hold onto the things they identified with the most – their self-importance, their narcissism – and they get on the bus and go back to that dreary life of sameness in hell. The teacher in the story boils it down this way: "There are only two kinds of people in the end: those who say to God, 'Thy will be done,' and those to whom God says, in the end, '*Thy* will be done.' All that are in Hell, choose it. Without that self-choice there could be no Hell."[23]

Lewis's book helped Polkinghorne appreciate that life is the unfolding exploration of divine nature, and it continues after we die. It shows the fulfilling of our ultimate destiny, which is to share in the infinite riches of that nature, moving toward infinite light. "It imaginatively conveys truth through story," he said. *The Great Divorce* reiterated for Polkinghorne the importance of how we live our lives today, especially in regard to whether we turn toward God or away from God. "Every turning away from

God will make the return journey that much the harder."[24]

The unhappy residents of hell are not there because they have been imprisoned by an angry God, fed up with offering mercy and forgiveness, Polkinghorne said. "The tragedy of hell is much worse than that, for they are there because they have chosen to be there. As the preachers say, the doors of hell are locked on the inside, its gates barred by its inhabitants to keep out the bright light of the saving divine presence."[25]

Christians in the nineteenth century began to rethink the traditional picture of hell as a place of infinite punishment for finite human sins. This horrific picture, which Charles Darwin found so repugnant it pushed him away from his childhood faith, was drawn as much from Dante's *Divine Comedy* as it was from a few select verses from Revelation. "I think that questioning was a Spirit-inspired move, leading to a much needed correction of distorted theological thinking. I am glad that we no longer picture hell in the way that seemed so natural and unproblematic to Dante."[26] The real meaning of the Fall, and of sin, and of hell, is in alienation from God, and the mistaken idea that we can truly live without his divine grace. "Hell is the place where that mistake continues to be made for ever. It is the setting of an unremitting refusal to allow ourselves ever to attain to the fulfillment of the true humanity that God intends for us."[27] Perhaps hell will have some inhabitants, but there is also the chance that it will be empty. Polkinghorne believes that thinking about hell as the place of eternal torment has been largely abandoned. "This has come about, not through surrender to a secular sentimentality, but through the realization of its incompatibility with the mercy of a loving God, who cannot be conceived to exact infinite punishment for finite wrong. Theology has proved itself to be open to correction."[28]

Polkinghorne's thinking about the world to come is driven by four propositions:

1. If the universe is a creation, and is still in the process of

being created, then that creative process will continue forever, beyond what happens to the material world that will either collapse in on itself or expand so much that it will be too cold for life.

2. If human beings are loved by their creator, then there must be a destiny beyond their deaths, which will include all previous generations, healed of their hurts, restored to their original purpose, participating in the divine purpose.

3. The information-bearing pattern of each of us will continue beyond death, but it will be free from the suffering and mortality of the old creation.

4. The ground for this hope is in the love and faithfulness of God that is revealed by the resurrection of Jesus.

Polkinghorne would try to communicate some of this as a vicar, when comforting those who had lost a loved one. "I would tell them that there was a destiny beyond death and that God was faithful and that nothing good was lost in the Lord," he said. Later he might try to discuss this more conjectural or intellectual account. "It's a delicate relationship between priest and parishioner. But ultimately you have to bear witness to what you think is true."

Even today he is careful in talking with a grieving person, and prays for discernment. "You still have to consider what the person is capable of hearing," he said. "Mostly, the point is to avoid talking too much, to be with the person silently. And one certainly must avoid saying, 'I can explain this – it's all about information-bearing patterns!'"

When the world does end, either through the Big Crunch or the Big Freeze, "At some such moment, the 'matter' of the dying cosmos will be changed into the 'matter' of the new creation, just as Jesus' dead body, in an unimaginable process about which the gospels are silent, was transformed into his risen and glorious body. That cosmic Day of Resurrection will be also the event in which the soul-patterns of all human beings, which have been held in the divine memory, will be reconstituted as embodied beings living in the new creation. Human destiny beyond death and cosmic destiny beyond death lie together."[29] This is why he still prays for those who have died. "When I pray for Ruth and for my brother and sister and parents, I feel the unity in Christ. I sometimes think the dead also pray for us. These slightly wacky notions must be taken seriously. I have reticence about people saying they felt the presence of someone who died. Heaven is a different dimension of reality. It's not a place. It's alongside us in the same way the Lord's presence is in the sacraments. The veil between the divine reality and the created reality is thinned."

It may seem strange that a physicist thinks and writes about something as unseen and unknowable as what happens at the end of this life, but it's a question scientists consider all of the time. Their study of how the universe began naturally leads them to consider how it will end – will gravity ultimately win out and have all material collapse in on itself, or will expansion win out and cool the universe so that it can no longer sustain life? Scientists and theologians alike have interest in the question of "And then what happens?"

"The proclamation by the sciences of the definite finitude of the world has come as a cultural shock. In the face of the environmental crisis, the continuing surge of global poverty, and the threat by an age of increasing conflict, scarcity and despair, many people around the world look to a future without hope or joy. The hard facts of life have shocked many from a naïve anthropocentrism wherein reality and reality's God exist to insure the fulfillment of the human project. A universe moving from big bang to heat death or cosmic crunch hardly seems to lend comfort to the human heart!"[30] Most cosmologists, when they peer into the future, see eventual futility, not fulfillment. That perspective leaves no room for a belief that "all will be well."

Polkinghorne responds to this bleak assessment with some of his favorite statements. The first is, "That's not the whole story," and the second is that discussion of the end of the world must have its basis of "trust in the everlasting faithfulness of the living and eternal God."[31] The faithfulness of God "is the only reality that can be set against the reality of the scientific predictions of catastrophe. Theology does not deny these predictions, but it transcends them. Christian hope is not a consoling fantasy that somehow death is an illusion. Death is real, but death is not ultimate. Only God is ultimate. The Christian hope is death and resurrection, not merely spiritual survival."[32]

Polkinghorne's views of Jesus' suffering and resurrection, as well as what happens after we die, are influenced by Jürgen Moltmann. Regarding death, Moltmann said, "I believe that God's history with our lives will go on after our deaths, until that completion has been reached in which a soul finds rest."[33] It is not a state of being, but a progression toward divine completion. Gregory of Nyssa said that the world to come is one of "unlimited progress toward perfection".[34]

In the world to come "what is brought about is the divine redemptive transformation of the old creation. The new is not a second creation... but it is a resurrected world. Involved in its coming to be must be both continuity and discontinuity, just as the Lord's risen body bears the scars of the passion but is also transmuted and glorified."[35]

In regard to continuity from this world to the next, Polkinghorne believes there will be a carryover of a "pattern," but we will be more than simply our individual selves as we experience them in this world. "The pattern that is me must include those human relationships that do so much to make me what I am, and also it must express the nature of my unique creaturely relationship with God."[36] The pattern that is Abraham, Isaac, and Jacob will really be those patriarchs, "not just new persons given the old names for old times' sake," Polkinghorne said. The pattern that is Polkinghorne and the patriarchs, and that is you and me, is our *soul*. But the soul is not just a detachable spiritual component that departs at death, like a helium balloon that gets loose of its string. The idea of the soul has to be "reconceptualized," he said. "Whatever it is, it is surely 'the real me,' carrying continuity in this life as much as beyond it... It will dissolve at death with the decay of the body, but it is a perfectly coherent belief that the faithful God will not allow it to be lost but will preserve it in the divine memory... Thus the ultimate Christian hope is resurrection, God's great eschatological act of the re-embodiment of information-bearing pattern in the environment of the new creation."[37]

Computer technology provides another way to look at the problem. The "software" that runs our "hardware" will be transferred to the hardware in the world to come, he said. That new hardware will come from the transformed matter we know in this world but will not be identical to it, just as the risen Jesus is the transformed Jesus who was crucified. "The resurrection of Jesus is the beginning within history of a process whose fulfillment lies beyond history, in which the destiny of humanity and the destiny of the universe are together to find their fulfillment in a liberation from decay and futility... What is to be will come from what is presently the case,"[38] and will involve "the endless, dynamic exploration of the inexhaustible riches of the divine nature."[39]

The Nobel Laureate Steven Weinberg, Polkinghorne's debate partner and friend, looks at the same evidence and finds the universe "pointless," "a farce". Francis Crick, who co-discovered the structure of DNA, says that there is nothing to the idea that an "information-bearing pattern" can carry on after life on earth. "You, your joys and your sorrows, your memories and your ambitions, your sense of personal identity and free will, are in fact no more than the behavior of a vast assembly of nerve-cells and their associated molecules."[40] But Polkinghorne thinks that such a conclusion is almost anti-scientific. "Science is built upon the foundation of the search for understanding and its reward is the sense of wonder induced by the discovery of the deep intelligibility of the universe, revealed in the rational beauty and rational transparency it is found to possess... The most astonishing event in cosmic history known to us – the emergence of persons by which the universe has become aware of itself – would be no more than a happy accident in a flux of absurdity."[41] This is why thinking about the end of the world is so important to Polkinghorne and why he believes it is an important topic for scientists in general. "Fundamentally, the issues center on the ultimate question, Does the universe make *complete* sense, not just now but always, or is it in the end, 'a tale told by an idiot, full of sound and fury, signifying nothing'?"[42]

But if God provides a world to come, why not just continue what was started here on earth? Why do we have to die? What is the grand purpose of that dreary and painful feature of our existence? From a physics standpoint, death exists because of the second law of thermodynamics, which says that ultimately disorder always triumphs over order. Everything heads inexorably downhill and ultimately to some kind of destruction. And in a world where its creatures have been empowered by God to make themselves through the evolutionary process, death must exist to make room for the next generation of life. "God's final intention," says Polkinghorne, "is the new creation drawn freely into such close connection with its Creator that its 'matter' suffused with the direct presence of a God no longer veiled, will permit the everlasting processes of eternal life."[43] It won't be a repetition of the world we just experienced, but neither will it be a slate wiped clean and a brand new world.

The life we lead now is separated by a veil from God. When we die we will be in a constant state of the unveiling of God, starting with judgment and purgation. "We're going to die in ignorance of ourselves. Judgment is not before an angry God, but seeing ourselves as we really are. Purgation is the washing away. Then we are more closely drawn into the brightness of the light. This will be forever, not ever in just one state."

Keith Ward and other scholars of the world's great religions have noted that many religious views connect the life to come with how it was lived in this world. The movement toward that brightness of light "should enable persons to see their earthly life in the wider context of the divine knowledge and experience of all things," Ward says. "It should enable people to recognize and come to terms with the evil they have done and perhaps to find some way of making amends for it. And it should enable persons to grow further in knowledge and love of the Supreme Good, in ways impossible on earth. In these ways, religious belief is bound up with the possibility of achieving an ultimate goal beyond the death of the body."[44]

Discussion of unseen realities are, of course, highly speculative. Despite his willingness to engage in such speculation, Polkinghorne acknowledges that the best view is to "wait and see". "Wait and see is not a bad motto, but we shouldn't lose our nerve about it. We're not mapping the geography of heaven. We should keep testing the consistency of the view. This is a thought experiment that we need to do, even though it may feel doubtful." Such thinking involves a degree of "flailing around," he admits, "but it's flailing around in the right direction. The information pattern of the soul will be re-embodied in God's great act of resurrection. This is an old idea of both Thomas Aquinas and Aristotle."

All of us die incomplete. It does not matter if we die peacefully at the end of a long productive life, or if we are struck down in our youth, the victim of neglect, war, famine, disease or a random act of violence. "If God is the Father of our Lord Jesus Christ, all the generations of oppressed and exploited people must have the prospect of a life beyond death, in which they will receive what was unjustly denied them in this life. Those who died in infancy, and those who died in the death camps, must have life restored to them." Those who never heard the gospel in a way they could embrace will have another opportunity in the life to come.[45] This is not a "happily ever after" ending, he maintains. To illustrate, he returns to the morality of literature.

"The death of the peasant boy in Ivan Karamazov's terrible story, deliberately torn in pieces before his mother's eyes by the hounds set upon him by the general whose dog he had accidentally injured, is not 'explained away' by his having a life beyond his awful death, but that death would have been even more terrible if it had led only to the grave. And, I think we must add, there is a deep human instinct that the murderous general must not escape answering for what he has done, even if justice is unable to touch him in this world."[46]

We die with lives incomplete, hurts unhealed, tasks unfinished, and with our sin unresolved. We die partly unrepentant, and with hearts in need of cleansing. Polkinghorne believes, "In the brighter light of the new creation we shall begin to see ourselves as we really are and as we are seen by God, and we shall have to come to terms with that painful reality. This is how I understand the serious matter of the judgment to come... We shall come to see how often we have preferred darkness to light."[47] The consequences won't be eternal punishment, but a purifying process, unfolding toward ultimate salvation.

But despite the cosmic tug of war between Crunch and Decay, Polkinghorne is filled with hope. The eventual futility of the universe, over a timescale of tens of billions of years, poses the same sort of theological problem raised by the eventual futility of ourselves, over a much shorter timescale of tens of years. "Cosmic death and human death pose equivalent questions of what is God's intention for his creation. What is at issue is the faithfulness of God, the everlasting seriousness with which he regards his creatures."[48]

"The picture of such a cosmic redemption, in which a resurrected humanity will participate, is both immensely thrilling and deeply mysterious. Yet its unimaginable future has a present anchorage in our hearts," says Polkinghorne. "There is a deep-seated intuition of hope, all the ambiguities and bitternesses of history notwithstanding, which encourages the belief that in the end all will be well."[49] Bishop John Robinson, who ordained Polkinghorne, said that a Christian "knows the present for what it is; that is to say, a point too charged with eternity to be understood except by myths which open a door into heaven and force upon every moment the terrible relevancy of the first things and the last, the elemental and the ultimate."[50]

As for what happens at the moment of death, Polkinghorne envisions two possibilities: God may hold the pattern that is us in his Divine Mind; or we may go directly to the day of resurrection, even though we all die at different times. Our sense of time today differs from what it will be "then". "It's hard to discern what the Scripture really says," he said. "Saying 'Wait and see' is not an intellectual cop-out. One can only use analogies to describe it, since it's an experience clearly different from any experience in this world."

With the death of Ruth, his brother, his parents, good friends, and those in parishes he has served, Polkinghorne often ponders the topic. "I pray that I will make a good death and that I will be delivered from the *fear* of death," he said. "One of the most important and significant episodes in the gospel is Jesus in the Garden of Gethsemane. As our redeemer, Christ experienced what we experience."

Chapter Eight
In Particular

One of John Polkinghorne's earliest memories is that of being pushed in a stroller by his mother and asking, "Where are we going?" It's an easy question for a toddler to ask and an easy one for his mother to answer. Most toddlers outgrow the need to ask this question, but little John Polkinghorne never did. Now eight decades after he rode about in that stroller, comfortable with the idea that his mother knew where they were going, he still asks that question.

He grew up pursuing both faith *and* science, and came to understand that the road that carries us to where we're going is much clearer if it is illuminated by both of them.

"Who has the better view of reality – faith or science?" he asks. "It's a false question. You have to be two-eyed about it. If we had only one eye, then we would say it's religion, because it relates to the deepest value of being human. Science doesn't plumb the depths that religion does."

Science, the other eye, is justifiably skeptical about religion, with its many competing claims and checkered history. Scientists want proof and religion seems short on that. Realistically, what can we prove about God? Polkinghorne is not put off by these concerns though.

"Proof in the strict sense of logic is a limited concept," he said. Even in math and science you don't always have proof. You can't know there isn't a lurking contradiction and there are historical examples where such contradictions appeared and sabotaged nice neat systems. "But that doesn't mean we're lost in a fog of ignorance" he says. There are a great many beliefs that are worth signing onto and, just because they cannot be absolutely proven, does not mean we should withhold our assent. On the other hand, there are those who demand a very high standard of proof – atheists for example – and are not prepared to sign on. Polkinghorne is inclined to be charitable toward those who cannot believe. "Atheists aren't stupid," he says. "They just explain less. They fail to grasp the argument."

A healthy understanding of the world takes both science and religion seriously. Polkinghorne's study of science, surprisingly, makes it *easy* for him to believe in God. In the first place, science has shown us that the universe is transparent and rationally beautiful but provided no answer for why it would be that way. That conclusion forces us to ask: Is that just our luck, or is there a reason for it? And when the Anthropic Principle, discussed in Chapter Five, shows that the universe is "just right" for life, with stars burning in a delicate balance that creates the chemical material necessary for our own lives, it seems like more than blind luck. There is harmony here between the scientific description of the world and the religious affirmation that this world is the product of a rational creator. Science and religion are not always in such harmony though.

There are examples of Christianity resisting the progress of science in history, to be sure. Who can forget that Galileo was confronted by the inquisition and censured for his belief that the earth moves about the sun? And we must certainly acknowledge the controversy surrounding the theory of evolution in today's world. But this is not the whole story. "Christianity was a major force in the development of scientific understanding," says Polkinghorne. The early scientists – Kepler, Galileo, Newton – were all convinced theists who believed that God was responsible for the underlying rationality of the world that they were discovering. "Our picture of God is not that he's just a mathematician," notes Polkinghorne, "but that our concept continues to enlarge and expand, even to a destiny beyond death." The "God as mathematician" metaphor, though, was very popular among the early scientists and may have encouraged their belief that there were important mathematical patterns to be discovered in nature.

When Polkinghorne left science to train for the priesthood, colleagues thought he was changing more than just his occupation. Many felt he was shutting down the part of his life dedicated to finding out how the world works, in physics, no less, where highly reliable knowledge could be obtained and theories could practically be proven in some cases. They also thought he was leaving physics to join a community of scholars of religion who pursued contentious and uncertain knowledge.

Polkinghorne, however, did not see it like this. While he did change the address of where he engaged in much of his thinking, some fundamental things remained unchanged, "among them a desire to understand the rich and complex world in which we live and to seek the truth about it."[1] His scientific inquiry had shown him how beautiful and elegant the natural world is; but it had also shown him how not everything has a nice, convenient explanation.

Quantum mechanics, the most philosophically provocative set of ideas in all of science, taught him that common sense could be an entirely misleading way to think about things. Why then, should we assume that religious ideas needed to conform to common sense? Just as the new physics was profoundly counter-intuitive, Polkinghorne was prepared for the truths of faith to be similar. Did this beautiful, elegant, transparent world have a meaning and purpose behind it? And, if so, could we find it? He decided to look for the evidence. As he studied Scripture and put his faith into practice, he felt that the evidence presented itself. "Christianity," he wrote in his first book, "affords a coherent insight into the strange way the world is."[2]

Scientists, especially early in their careers, rarely think like this: "Most scientists are philosophically unreflective," he said. "When I was a mathematician, I just got on with my job. Only when I started reading the philosophy of science, and theology, did I start leaning toward seminary. It was a change in my thinking – an enhancing change."

One might think that top scientists, whose ideas shape our worldviews, have clear ideas about truth and reality. But this is not the case, says Polkinghorne. "I studied under Dirac, but he was completely unreflective. Anything out of his central vision was not a concern of his." While religion is often described as a means for keeping one's spirits up and anesthetizing the pain of real life, or a way to keep the masses under control – which is the message of "The Grand Inquisitor" – Polkinghorne sees it as so much more: "The central religious question is the question of truth. Of course, religion can sustain us in life, or at the approach of death, but it can only do so if it is about the way things really are. Some of the people I know who seem to me to be the most clear-eyed and unflinching in their engagement with reality are monks and nuns, people following the religious life of prayerful awareness."[3]

As he pursued this, he wasn't interested in whether Christianity provided comfort in crisis or a stiff upper lip when facing life or death. His question was simply: Is it true? And if so, what does this truth imply about the details of the world? As with the existence of electrons, gluons, and quarks – none of which can be seen directly – the best one can do is create a theory and test it. "Part of my reason for being a Christian is that I believe that a Christian understanding offers us such a coherent framework adequate to the perplexing way the world is."[4]

Polkinghorne was searching for truth, both eyes open. "Religious people who are seeking to serve the God of truth should welcome all truth from whatever source it may come, without fear or reserve. Included in this open embrace must certainly be the truths of science. In the case of the scientists... they will have to be prepared to go beyond the limits of science itself in the search for the widest and deepest context of intelligibility. I think that this further quest, if openly pursued, will take the enquirer in the direction of religious belief. It is a search for the *Logos*."[5]

Still, it's not proof. "I have not been able to *prove* Christianity for you any more than you could demonstrate to me beyond a peradventure whatever view of the world you hold. When you come to think about it, there is very little of interest that is susceptible to that sort of proof."[6]

Polkinghorne's work in university settings has been in the field of the mind – experiments, theories, discoveries, mentoring, presiding over educational institutions. But being two-eyed about life is more than just a pursuit of the mind. "We are a great deal more than minds and a real view of the world will have to engage our whole personalities," he said. "That is why religions always speak of an act of faith, a response at the deepest levels of our being to that One who is the ground of our being."[7] Ultimately, the possibility of God and of a personal relationship with such a Being is not a philosophical position, or an intellectual hypothesis. It is a personal commitment. It involves faith. "I do not think that it is a question of shutting our eyes and hoping for the best in a blind lunge at reality. Of course we should look before we leap. Faith cannot be proved, but it is not unmotivated."[8]

It is a challenge to present this view to his friends – scientists or others – who simply don't have the same leanings toward faith. When he talks privately with physicist Steven Weinberg, for instance, the two disagree fundamentally about the existence of God and the possibility of faith. And yet, Polkinghorne said, Weinberg keeps bringing the subject up when they are together. But his disagreement with other scientists is about looking at the same information and drawing different conclusions. "What is at issue between us is the existence of a religious dimension to life, an experience of the Other, together with the credibility of a purpose in the world and a destiny for man beyond the commonly acknowledged circumstances of the way of the world... As far as purpose and destiny are concerned, we are reading the same facts in different ways."[9]

Perhaps even more challenging is whether the Christian faith is "true" in the context of other faiths. Most faiths include belief in a religious dimension to life, a purpose in the world, and a destiny for mankind. But the similarities soon break down. Is there only one right answer? Are all faiths equal in some abstract sense? In such discussions, one must acknowledge where one was raised. "It would be disingenuous to maintain that my being a Christian is totally unconnected with the fact that I was born in Britain," Polkinghorne said. "Had I been born in India the chances are I would be a Hindu. Had I been born in Saudi Arabia it would have been a virtual certainty that I would have been a Muslim. Is religion once again dissolving into a sea of culturally determined conflicting opinions?"[10]

If the discussion were primarily about lifestyle, then there wouldn't be much need for a resolution. Different cultures produce different lifestyles, which makes the tapestry of human experience so satisfying. The diversity of our interactions in the world keeps things interesting. But differences in religions are more than differences in lifestyle. Differences in religion lead to significantly different views of ultimate reality.

There is no question, Polkinghorne believes, that God is truly experienced in other faiths. The view of some Christian groups that other faiths by definition are in error, is simply wrong. "It implies the extraordinary conclusion that God has left himself without witness in the world at most times and in most places," he said. "If the Word is the light that enlightens every man, that would be an intolerable conclusion to reach.

It is also contrary to our observation. Across the cultural gaps and the differences that divide us, we can discern in some adherents of other faiths a holiness and depth of experience which commands our silent respect and recognition."[11]

Polkinghorne recalls watching a television program on world faiths. The interviewer, Ronald Eyre, who had also interviewed Polkinghorne for a different program, was interviewing a Buddhist Zen master. "Through the medium of television there was a spiritual authenticity that was undeniable," he said. "He was living in the presence of God. You simply can't say, 'poor chap – he doesn't know anything.' Bottom-up thinking says there is something there."

He cites Vincent Donovan and Matteo Ricci as examples of missionaries who took Christianity to other cultures. They worked first to honor and respect the cultures they were in, and thus came to appreciate the faiths of these civilizations. Donovan worked in Tanzania among the Masai tribe in the 1960s, and his book *Christianity Rediscovered* recounts his seeing the work of God among the Masai, helping them bear witness to the spirit of Christ already present. Ricci lived in China in the late 1500s and early 1600s, and took Western science with him. Christianity flourished in China because of Ricci's ability to find common ground with the Chinese. "I am similar in this way to those missionaries," said Polkinghorne. "I don't want to compromise, but I can't just go in and say 'Here it is.'"

But sometimes the differences loom too large to ignore the chasm between religions. In regard to Buddhism, he says, "I cannot accept that the suffering of the world is an illusion from which release is to be sought by enlightenment. Rather, the cross of Christ demonstrates the objective and inescapable character of that suffering. A Buddhist might find a crucifix an ugly and degrading symbol of suffering. I believe that on the cross Jesus opened his arms to embrace the bitterness of the world."[12] As for differences between Christianity and Islam or Judaism, the fundamental issue is the significance of Jesus. It isn't enough, Polkinghorne believes, to merely be sensitive to the teachings of Jesus. Gandhi felt that the Sermon on the Mount was more important than whether Jesus actually existed. "The Christian gospel is not primarily concerned with good advice but with salvation, an act of power by God to redeem the marred character of humanity. It centres on the God-man Jesus as the unique meeting of God's love and man's need. If he did not exist Christianity collapses."[13]

All human hope has its origin in Jesus, he said, firmly planting his flag. Other religions may have important insights that could improve our Christian practice, but it is the *particularity* of Jesus that Polkinghorne finds compelling. Without Jesus as a historical figure whose resurrection began a New Creation, then Christian faith would not be credible.[14] Other faiths have particulars, too, including the Buddha, the Koran, Mohammed, and the Torah. Their particulars are more than surface differences. The Abrahamic faiths of Christianity, Islam, and Judaism portray individual human life as unique with lasting significance. The Hindu faith has human life recycled through reincarnation. The Buddhist faith sees life as an illusion from which to seek release. Can these differing views just be different ways of having similar religious views? "These conflicting concepts do not seem to be culturally different ways of expressing the same idea."[15] And if they aren't saying the same thing, and they're saying that each is true, what then? "It does not seem that all these claims can simultaneously be true, as though they were simply culturally moulded expressions of the same fundamental insight."[16] This poses a major challenge to people of faith.

Second only to the problem of suffering and evil, the reality of the world's varying faiths is the top reason people reject Christianity, Polkinghorne said. One of the differences among the faiths is their view of human nature:

I am deeply perplexed by that, and it is worrying.
People used to consider other religions weird and a
world away. Now they are down the street and live
with integrity. We have to talk seriously about them
and find meeting places. But you can't start at the
center. We do have similar stories about the arrival
of evil, and of creation, and of a great flood. But
the answer does not lie in finding the lowest common
denominator. That is too anemic. I do not do others
a service by not mentioning Jesus. Otherwise we are
papering over our differences. Don't let's pretend
that we don't have serious differences.

And some of these differences are substantial: "That there should be diversities of religious understanding is not surprising; that the discrepancies in the accounts of ultimate reality are so great, is very troubling."[17] However, even when the differences lead to intolerance and violence, that doesn't negate what is valued by the majority within those faiths, he said.[18]

All religions have a sense of the sacred, and mystics from different faiths give similar testimonies regarding their experiences and insights in regard to a sacred reality. They also share an emphasis on compassion. But what about those differences?

One fundamental difference between Christianity and Buddhism, for instance, is in the view of the Self. Buddhism has a doctrine of *non-self*, because individualism is at heart an *illusion*, and it leads to suffering. And while Jesus tells his followers to deny themselves to follow him, he is talking about realigning the impure desire of the ego with the right desire, "that seeking of the soul for God which is central to the thought of Augustine, that dart of longing love by which the Christian mystic seeks to penetrate the Cloud of Unknowing." The value of human individuality is central to this belief.[19] Some faith traditions focus on the bankruptcy of man, and the need to escape from our humanity. Polkinghorne believes that the Christian tradition celebrates the glory of humanity.

Another difference relates to the view of time. Christianity is rooted in linear history, while some faiths see time as an illusion. All faith traditions, not surprisingly, have difficulty in talking about God. Most have writings that provide illumination and authority. "Part of the ecumenical encounter of the world faiths must involve decisions about how they are to view each other's sacred writings."[20] Polkinghorne gives priority to the New Testament, because of the unique role of Christ in it, but the Old Testament also has priority since it was the Scripture used by Jesus and the disciples. But, since the canon of the Bible does not include writings from other parts of the world, such as India, he is open to what else might be significant. "My inclusivist stance equally implies that I may expect to find passages of spiritual value, including, doubtless, insights not to be found elsewhere, in the other scriptures of the world."[21] Still, while he has appreciation and openness to other sacred writings, "I have to say personally that they do not speak to me as the Bible does... I have to confess to considerable reservations about occasions of interfaith worship in which common denominator lessons are read. I think the faiths have to meet each other in the strangeness of their differences, and if any common form of worship is attempted it might well be best conducted in a shared meditative silence."[22]

The biggest sticking point, of course, is Jesus. Most faiths recognize Jesus as an important teacher and prophet, but would not call him the unique incarnation of God in humanity. The Koran calls Jesus a messenger from God, but says he did not die on the cross. "Not only is this notion totally unhistorical, but it also is in contradiction with the profound and fundamental insight of Christianity that the cross of Christ represents God's solidarity with us as a 'fellow sufferer.' This literally crucial issue is one that any realistic inter-faith dialogue will have to face."[23] The Buddhist view of Jesus crucified is also a stumbling block, because being crucified is bad karma. Buddhists do not factor in salvation through vicarious suffering. "The typical Buddhist symbol is that of the serene and smiling Buddha, seated in the lotus position – not a man on the gallows."[24]

Hinduism, and its tenet of reincarnation, is troublesome. "Reincarnation offers a tactical solution to the problem of how individual suffering is distributed, but not a strategic solution to the problem of why there is a world so constituted as to have so much suffering in it."[25]

Interfaith dialogue is problematic as long as one of the group claims it possesses a vital truth. Truth is always divisive, theologians say, until it becomes universal. "I sometimes fear that Christianity is a little too eager for dialogue, a little lacking in nerve to hold fast to what it has learned of God in Christ. We Europeans must shake off lingering guilt arising from our colonial past. We certainly do not want to be triumphalist, but nor do we wish to forget that there may well be issues on which we are right and those who do not share our view are mistaken. In the end, it is that question of truth that matters, and there is an inevitable exclusivity about truth."[26] If, for example, a person views heat as something other than kinetic energy, it would not be useful to say to that person, "You are entitled to your own opinion."

> *Either Jesus is God's Lord and Christ or he is*
> *not, and it matters supremely to know which is the*
> *right judgment. Of course, we must be careful to*
> *distinguish between the necessary intolerance that*
> *truth has of error and a social intolerance exhibited*
> *by failing to respect as people those whose opinions*
> *we believe to be mistaken... We can conduct our*
> *dialogue both with respect and to the point...*
> *A religion which has resisted its own dissolving into*

> *a gnostic account of timeless truth should be open
> to meeting the historic idiosyncrasies present in all
> religious traditions, without reducing them to merely
> contingent collections of opinion.*[27]

Polkinghorne acknowledges that truth always contains an element of intolerance. "If you believe Jesus, then you can't help but think that the others have missed something," he said. "It implies a superiority, but you can't despise them for it. If you tell me that the earth is 6,000 years old, I have a superior view. If x is true, and y contradicts x, then y is a mistaken point of view." That doesn't mean we can't learn from other faiths, though. Other faiths provide insights and experiences that those in the Christian faith might not have. Thomas Merton, the Trappist monk, had a famous deep relationship with Buddhist monks of Southeast Asia. "But that's not the same as saying Christianity is just an option," Polkinghorne said.

But just because one may believe in Jesus doesn't mean interfaith dialogue should start there. "You can't start with Jesus," he said. "I don't do anyone any favours by disguising the status of Jesus in my life, but you can't throw this in their faces, or we just fire from our trenches. You have to say what someone can hear. There were a couple of chaps in the market square of Cambridge who would thump their Bibles and preach to people walking by. They brought the gospel into contempt. They said things that were true, but in ways most people won't be able to hear."

Interfaith dialogue is just beginning to occur at a serious level, he said, but he cautioned about both the pace and the content of that dialogue. Think centuries, rather than years, he warns. "We've made progress, but just a small bit. It's a long, complicated business, but I don't get discouraged by the slowness."

For Polkinghorne, Jesus is more than his local icon. He is the bridge from the life of God to humanity. That's Polkinghorne's sacred reality. "We need a way of proceeding that neither denies that all traditions preserve true reports of encounter with sacred reality nor seeks to smooth over their individual differences. I feel that I have to approach such a dialogue from the perspective of my Trinitarian belief. To do otherwise would be disingenuous, and I expect my brothers and sisters in other faith traditions also to speak from where they are."[28] Not discussing the centrality of Jesus "would be as misleading on my part as it would be for a Muslim to try to conceal belief in the unique status of the Koran. Our differing beliefs in these respects are why the process of ecumenical dialogue will inevitably be long and painful, and why it has to begin with matters not too intrinsically threatening. What it will eventually lead to is not foreseeable today."[29]

Polkinghorne is also sensitive to finding such a low common denominator that the discussion becomes irrelevant, "so rarified in content that virtually no adherent of any faith tradition would consider them worthy of assenting to, or even worth arguing about."[30]

But there are meaningful interfaith conversations to be had. The topics include each tradition's view of the nature of the physical world and our relationship to it; how evolution relates to the different creation accounts; whether the intelligibility of mathematics points to a cosmic Mind; whether the anthropic fine-tuning of the laws of nature indicate a cosmic purpose; how the insights of physiology, psychology, and philosophy affect the view of the human self; the significance of science's prediction of eventual cosmic collapse or decay; how the bottom-up (evidence-based) thinking of science affects religious claims.[31] In other words, the place to begin interfaith dialogue could be in science.

Science differs from faith in part because everyone can get the same answers to scientific questions, regardless of where in the world the question is posed. "Ask a suitably qualified person in Rome or Jerusalem, Benares or Kyoto, what matter is made of, and in all four cities you will receive the same reply, 'quarks and gluons.' Ask four people in those four cities what is the nature of ultimate reality, and their answers will likely be very divergent, " he notes.[32] "I believe that initial occasions of meeting will have to address serious questions, but that immediate and direct engagement with the core defining beliefs of each tradition (What about Jesus? What about the Koran?), if undertaken prematurely, would be likely to prove too threatening on all sides for progress to be made. One possible fruitful field of encounter can be afforded by the faiths sharing their insights into how they understand the discoveries of modern science to relate to their traditional theological understandings."[33]

It is not helpful, he believes, and not even in his nature, to assert a superior position. "I reject the notion that we Christians know everything and that all the others are just plain wrong. Religious people can no more neglect the challenge of the multiplicity of the world faiths than the physicists could neglect light's duality of wave and particle."[34]

During his college days as a member of the Christian Union, other faiths were barely on the radar and, if they were, they had a little flag "wrong" attached to them. "It was very narrow back then – they weren't even sure about Roman Catholics," he said. "But you eventually have to come out of that world. It's too narrow. When Jesus says 'I am the Way,' he's not talking about just this life. There is a post-mortem fulfillment."

True ecumenical dialogue occurs only when people of other faiths meet with humility, not in a head-on collision, Polkinghorne said. The necessity of witnessing to the truth as one understands it is the issue. He uses physics as an example of how to do this. "If you were to tell me that you believe that Isaac Newton was absolutely right in absolutely every respect in his understanding of mechanics and gravitation, I would not reply, 'Don't be silly,' nor would I say, 'That's very interesting and I respect your opinion.' Instead, I would try, tactfully but firmly, to explain why I believe that Newton's profound insights need modification and amplification in the light of the further discoveries of relativity and quantum theory. This must surely be similar in the religious search for truthful belief."[35]

Polkinghorne identifies three broad approaches to religious diversity. One is a pluralism that declares all faiths have equal standing and validity – they are just different ladders up the same wall. He allows that salvation is available to all, but rejects the equality of all viewpoints. "Christianity is the most intellectual of all the faiths because it has the study of theology, and theology is not a part of all faiths," he said. Jewish faith is more concerned with the ethical, practical side of how we live our lives than it is with intellectual issues regarding faith. "Muslims can tell you what the Koran says, but not all find it easy to probe the intellectual issues of its interpretation. It's not structured into their faith," he said. When Polkinghorne speaks publicly on matters regarding science and religion, he is often approached by people with Islamic or Jewish backgrounds, who affirm that they share his views on how the universe can be understood in terms of theology, and on his views of creation.

The second interfaith option is for each group to claim it has the truth and everyone else is mistaken. Several Christian philosophers have labeled people of other faiths "anonymous Christians," or Christians who don't know they're Christians. That approach "has sometimes been seen as a patronizing or imperialistic way of speaking, but the basic concept, rightly construed as the implicit presence of the Word and the covert activity of the Spirit throughout the breadth of the human religious quest, can be freed from those undesirable overtones".[36] And while Polkinghorne believes that Christianity is true, he is careful, and even a bit ambiguous, in how he says it.

"Am I comfortable with ambiguity?" he said. "I'm more uncomfortable with spurious clarity. Almost all reductionist accounts chop off the ends that don't fit. Daniel Dennett does it. For him, introspection has no role. It's a popular, manageable package and it's successful, but it's implausible. Dawkins does the same. His genetic survival machine includes only part of the argument. You have to be an extraordinarily diminished person to live out that attitude." Christianity, on the other hand, is often reduced to a faith concerned only with the saving of souls. "It would be a crude notion of how God deals with humanity to say it's only about saving souls," Polkinghorne said. "Jesus did not insist on prior repentance when spending time with sinners."

Polkinghorne's experience as a physicist makes him comfortable with ambiguity, and the notion that there is always more to the story. "In 1900, physicists only knew about the wave aspect of light, but they suspected there was something else," he said. "Physicists had to live with the ambiguity until it could be resolved. It teaches us a lesson to hang on."

A third interfaith option is more inclusive, where the commitment is to pursuing truth, even as it encourages dialogue. "An inclusivist position confers no monopoly of truth on any tradition, and therefore it encourages dialogue between the traditions... Each tradition may expect enhancement and correction from the others" without denying that there are different degrees of completeness in the insights that they offer, and Christians should not be surprised by the Holy Spirit's conviction coming from a different faith.[37] If truth is the pursuit, the Holy Spirit is at work in *any* truth-seeking community, including scientists. "That's part of the generosity of God," he said. The search for truth is ultimately the search for God.[38]

Eventually the Spirit of God will mitigate these differences, he says. He believes this because of the precedent of the Holy Spirit's movement as told in Acts 2. "The outpouring of the Spirit drew together those who were culturally and linguistically diverse in the Pentecostal reversal of Babel."[39]

Meanwhile, God remains elusive, veiled and beyond comprehension. "That is the way the world is. God does not shrivel us by the bright beam of his glory but he allows his light to diffuse and be refracted by the myriad cultural prisms of men."[40]

Interfaith dialogue occurs in the growing recognition that human attempts to connect to God are as old as the first self-aware animals. It was this primordial religious impulse, predating the appearance of any particular religion that developed into the collection of religions in the world today.

"Ancient civilizations had their tales of the gods come among men. Part of the attraction of modern science fiction, with its talk of other worlds and other beings, is that it ministers to the sublimated desire we have to be in touch with someone from outside the confined world of men. The talking animals of children's stories are another aspect of the same desire. There is a deep feeling within man that he is not complete without Another and there is a deep longing for that Other to make himself known. We are thirsty for God." The concrete, historical figure of Jesus of Nazareth doesn't explain the world, but it shows how God is involved and identifies with the contradictions of the world. "Both the pain and the hope that are in the world need to find their place in its understanding. They meet in the cross and resurrection of Jesus. To me this Christian world view has the mark of truth, a coherence, a degree of realism and an adequate complexity, which match the strange way the world is."[41]

But scientists never think just about the past, or even just the present known world. What if there was life elsewhere, too, that we haven't yet discovered? What if science fiction writers have been on to something all along that scientists haven't been able to verify? "What if there are intelligent beings elsewhere in the universe, perhaps possessing powers of understanding orders of magnitude beyond that which humans are capable of attaining?" he said. "Science does not really know what to think about this extraterrestrial possibility." Suppose primitive life – a bacterium, for instance – is discovered. What if it could become more complex through evolution, resulting in self-conscious beings? "There must surely be many sites in the universe suitable for the development of some form of life, but until we understand the biochemical pathways by which this has happened on Earth, we do not know how likely it is actually to occur elsewhere," Polkinghorne said.

> *Distinguished scientists disagree radically about this, so we may conclude that the question remains unsettled. Theology does not altogether know what to think about extraterrestrial possibilities, either. God's creative purposes may well include 'little green men' as well as human, and if they need redemption we may well think that the Word would take little green flesh just as we believe the Word took our flesh. If we ever do make contact with intelligent life elsewhere, that will be of great significance both scientifically (do they have the same genetic code as us?) and theologically (what are their religious experiences and beliefs?).[42]*

Scientists also ask speculative questions about life on earth in the future. The average lifetime of a species is a few million years. Is it possible that Homo sapiens could eventually evolve into a superior being, with physical and intellectual powers exceeding that of present civilization? Polkinghorne believes it is reasonable to think about a species yet to come, just as our own appearance as self-conscious beings developed from our ancestors. "Are we not in danger of being presumptuously premature in our thinking, unjustifiably inflating the significance of our current form of particularity?" he asks. Polkinghorne is clearly energized by these questions, but he doesn't lose sight of what he believes is most important – the present, what we know, here on earth. "As a Christian who believes that God took human life in Jesus Christ, I inevitably think that there must be something of particular significance in present humanity... This specific universe is a creation endowed with a rational order that is accessible to creatures who are made in the image of the Creator."[43]

Those creatures often do things, though, that seem out of synch with a loving creator. And many times they do them in the name of religion. Polkinghorne is challenged frequently about whether religion inspires evil acts. The Spanish Inquisition comes to mind, along with the Salem Witch Trials. "Any religious person has to acknowledge with regret and penitence that evil acts have been done in the name of religion. The sad history of crusades and inquisitions makes the point. One must also recognize the many good and fruitful acts of care and compassion that religion has inspired, as well as much creativity in music and the arts." Hitler, Pol Pot, and Stalin did not have religious ties, however. "The truth of the matter is that evil acts arise neither from religion nor lack of religion, as such, but from an inherent flaw in human nature that often turns a country's liberator into its next tyrant... It is a wise saying that 'the corruption of the best is the worst'. When religion goes wrong, it can do so in very destructive ways, but this is a distortion of its true inspiration."[44]

Christians, Jews, and Muslims have all used the messages in their holy books as justification to slaughter each other. "The sword has played a significant role in all of their histories," he said. "But there is also a history of tolerating people. All paths have dark sides to their histories. That's the mistake Dawkins makes – he says all bad things come from religions, when it's really human nature he's talking about."

In reflecting on the grand questions that religions ponder, Polkinghorne is convinced that strong reasons support three encouraging conclusions:

1. Belief in God is rational. Such a belief *might* be incorrect, but it's not a "delusion".

2. No real conflict exists between science and Christianity, though there are unanswered questions about how they relate, just as there are unanswered questions about the relationship among different sciences.

3. Most objects in the universe are not just machines set in motion after the Big Bang and running on their own. "In particular, science does not require us to believe that we do not have free will."[45] We live in a world of true becoming, where the future is *not* just an inevitable consequence of the past.[46]

Of all branches of science, quantum physics could be the most compatible with belief in God, because quantum physicists are comfortable with counter-intuitive thinking. More traditional classical physicists think in terms of the machine universe, black and white, wave or particle, no ambiguity.

"If the study of quantum physics teaches one anything, it is that the world is full of surprises... As Haldane once said, the world is not only stranger than we thought; it is stranger than we could think... Even logic has to be modified when it is applied to the quantum world."[47] And logic will only take us so far. "To be frank, we do not have as tight an intellectual grasp of quantum theory as we would like to have. We can do the sums and, in that sense, explain the phenomena, but we do not really *understand* what is going on."[48]

The great physicist Niels Bohr also said that there are two kinds of truth – items so trivial that embracing their opposites would be absurd, and items so profound that their opposite is also a profound truth. "The essential thing about seeming paradox, whether in science or in theology, is that it should be forced upon us by experience and not just embraced in a fit of unrestrained speculative exuberance."[49]

The biggest ambiguity of all, though, might be that all our scientific knowledge is based on the inspection of a tiny portion of the observable universe. Seventy-six percent of the material in the universe is considered dark energy. Twenty percent is considered dark matter. That leaves just four percent that's observable. Is it crazy to base so much on so little, when *almost everything is unknowable,* at least at present?

"We know something about dark energy and matter," Polkinghorne said. "We have well-motivated conjectures. The fact that there is such a small observable part is precarious. But even if it's just four percent, we should take all truth seriously. Four percent is not to be despised."

And, as he frequently admits, our understanding of science, the universe, God, might be all wrong.

"But what else can you do?" he said. "There is the mystery of God, the strangeness of God. Nevertheless, we hold on."

Conclusion: Icon

John Polkinghorne awakens in his quiet neighborhood between 6 and 6.30 in the morning. His days since retiring from the Queens' College presidency have involved travel around the world speaking on the compatibility between faith and science, but when he is home in Cambridge, he sticks to a routine. He eats a simple breakfast in his kitchen and says the Daily Office. He is usually in his study by 8 a.m., a room packed floor to ceiling with more books than are found in many science or theology libraries. On one table are stacks of paper – manuscripts he's agreed to review, chapters he's agreed to write, drafts of speeches he's agreed to give. A recent tally showed eleven different projects silently lobbying for his attention that day.

A pad of legal-sized paper sits on another table. Polkinghorne writes his book manuscripts longhand on those pads, then puts them away for a few months. Eventually he retrieves them from a pile and types them on his computer – the only time he uses his computer. His fax machine, in contrast, rings and churns throughout the day. One recent day saw a fax arrive from Yale University Press asking him to approve the cover of one of his books they are publishing. Another was from a different university press compiling a "John Polkinghorne Reader". Another came from Germany regarding details of a talk he would be giving there soon. The BBC called. And on it goes – a day in the life of John Polkinghorne.

He stops writing around noon, and drives out of his quiet neighborhood, avoiding streets clogged with driving instructors teaching young people the rules of the road, and heads to Queens' College. As a former president he has a coveted parking place at Queens'. He walks up a flight of stairs and enters a familiar room through a high, thick door. Inside is a long table where Queens' professors have gathered over the decades for lunch. This is no college cafeteria, though, with overcooked pasta and stewed tomatoes. The buffet-style food at Queens' is an experience in fine dining.

On this particular day the mostly male professors were discussing the interviews they had been conducting. This was the annual interview season, when students hoping to attend a University of Cambridge college come for a few days to try to impress the professors enough to be admitted. Judging by the conversations at this particular table, most of the students interviewing at Queens' College that day will be going home disappointed.

After lunch Polkinghorne heads next door to the Senior Combination Room for a finishing cup of coffee. The room is full of small tables, where other faculty drink coffee and tea, discuss the day's events, and read the newspaper. On one wall is a painting of the Queen Mother, commemorating her visit to Queens'. Other walls hold large portraits of past presidents, including Polkinghorne. The windows overlook the River Cam where students and tourists are trying to navigate in narrow, flat boats called punts.

Across the river is the building where Polkinghorne used to live, the President's Lodge. It is where he designed the crest for his presidency, imprinted with what has become one of his favorite Scripture verses – 1 Thessalonians 5:21 "Test everything: hold fast to what is good" (ESV)

After lunch, and back at his house, he picks up his writing where he left off and works until mid-afternoon. Then he reads theology for a few hours. He has a light dinner, and relaxes in the evening.

On some Wednesday mornings he is at the Good Shepherd

Anglican Church. It's a five-minute walk from his house, past a playground and a grocery store. He celebrates the Eucharist with those in the parish who are able to attend, and leads them in reciting the Nicene Creed. And when Revd John Polkinghorne says "I believe in one God the Father almighty, maker of heaven and earth, and of all things visible and invisible," he's not just showing what he memorized as a child. He knows what he's talking about.

A few times a year he meets with a spiritual director. It's a practice he started when he first became a priest. His first spiritual director was a retired Anglican bishop, and they talked mostly about spiritual disciplines. It was practical in its nature. When he was in Blean, he met with a vicar from a different parish. Again, it was practical, sometimes about awkward people in their parishes. When he moved back to Cambridge he met with a lecturer on spirituality – a former Roman Catholic priest who taught at the Westcott Seminary. When that lecturer moved away, he recommended that Polkinghorne meet with a sister from the Community of Jesus, an organization started in the seventeenth century as the female counterpart to the Jesuits.

This sister is a former Anglican, who became a Roman Catholic nun after her husband was killed in World War II. She's in her eighties, a few years older than John. They talk about the complexities of life, of losing a spouse, of loneliness, of the desire to make a good death.

Spiritual directors are like mirrors. They are usually wise and insightful, and make people think deeply about themselves. Directors are similar to therapists, but one sees a spiritual director less frequently, and spiritual directors are much more deliberate in giving advice. Spiritual directors give a person an occasion to review, evaluate and confess in privacy.

Without intending to be, Polkinghorne himself is a spiritual director to countless scientists, priests, students, and parishioners around the world. Through his teaching, writing, speaking, and friendships, he assists those who lack certainty – which is most of us – to test everything, and hold fast to what is true.

When John Polkinghorne left physics to enter the priesthood, much of his early theological training occurred in the chapel at Westcott Seminary. It's a plain chapel, compared to other chapels and churches in Cambridge. It seats about thirty, as opposed to the hundreds, even thousands, that can fill cathedrals. No stunning architecture animates Westcott. No high ceilings gather the pipe organ's notes to fly around and echo. In fact, there is no pipe organ in this chapel. There are no large and famous paintings, like there are in the other chapels. No stained glass windows tell New Testament stories, as there are even right across the street. The benches at Westcott don't have hand carvings of the apostles in the ends. They're just plain, humble benches, unpretentious and functional.

No dazzling sounds, no dazzling lights, no dazzling sights. Just one candle lit, illuminating the icon that Polkinghorne and his classmates commissioned years ago. It is the face of Jesus, and he's saying, "You have not chosen me. I have chosen you."

Occasionally John Polkinghorne walks through the wooden door of Westcott Seminary, past the small, manicured quad, past the small, simple library, and into the chapel. He sits quietly, gazes at the icon in the silence, knows he is not alone, knows why he is there, and feels at home.

Epilogue

Participants filed into the University of Oxford's Martin Wood Lecture Theatre with anticipation. For four days they had been discussing the cosmos, the nature of the universe, relativity, chaos theory, string theory, critical realism, philosophy, nature, theology, the end of the world, the Trinity, the character of God, divine action – in other words, the roster of topics that John Polkinghorne has been writing about for decades. More than fifty speakers from around the world had presented on Polkinghorne-related topics during this event titled "God and Physics." They took his ideas and explored them under their own intellectual microscopes, and sometimes expanded them into something greater. It was a commemoration of Polkinghorne's contributions to the dialogue involving science and religion, and a celebration of his eightieth birthday.

Physicists, philosophers, theologians, chemists, biologists, priests, and professors from England, the United States, Canada, Norway, Ireland, Italy, Israel, India, Uganda, Mexico, Germany, Scotland, Japan, Korea, and the Netherlands were there. Some were former students of Polkinghorne's at Cambridge. Some were colleagues. Some taught whole courses at their own universities based on his work. Some just wanted to be in the same place as the person who, through his books, had rescued them from the uncomfortable spot between the rock of faith and the hard place of science.

The audience stirred even more when Richard Harries entered the lecture hall. Harries is a former bishop in the Church of England at Oxford, and member of the House of Lords. He and Polkinghorne greeted one another with enthusiasm.

It was fitting that the event took place at the Clarendon Laboratory building at Oxford, where a great deal of research had been done on the development of lasers – our most powerful source of illumination. Another form of illumination had been occurring for the previous few days. Light that illuminated how the search for truth involves evidence as well as motivation, seen and unseen realities; light making it possible to see the world's endless surprises.

The area has seen both significant scientific discoveries *and* enduring works of the imagination, both of which reveal the beauty and creativity of the universe. Just a few blocks from the Clarendon Laboratory is the Eagle and Child pub, where C. S. Lewis, J. R. R. Tolkien, and other "Inklings" would read each other's work and spur each others' imaginations. A ten-minute walk takes one from Clarendon to Magdalen College, where Lewis taught and Oscar Wilde studied. The Deer Park is part of the landscape there, and it inspired other great literature. The Harry Potter movies were filmed in other university buildings nearby. The great science writer and infamous atheist Richard Dawkins lives just down the street. Shakespeare's Stratford-upon-Avon and the beautiful Cotswolds are within easy reach.

Polkinghorne was comfortable addressing the intellectuals who had gathered to honor him in Oxford. This group wasn't hostile. In fact, he knew he was among friends. He loves to talk about what it means to be both a serious scientist and a person of faith. For him, it's all about evidence. Mastering quantum physics is the perfect training ground for studying theology, in his view, because it's the evidence that leads a physicist to believe in the equations, and it's the evidence that leads a person of faith to believe in God. Polkinghorne's term for this old-fashioned approach is "bottom-up thinking". This is different from starting with settled beliefs (whether in science or faith) and then searching for evidence to support those beliefs.

Bottom-up evidence leads one to draw conclusions.

Polkinghorne will talk about this with anyone – parishioners in Blean, Nobel Prize-winning atheists, university audiences, the queen, and small church groups. One conference attendee recalled starting a science/religion discussion group in his church, and they read some of Polkinghorne's work. The man wrote to Polkinghorne and asked if he'd be willing to meet with his group. "I can't pay you, but I can offer you my home to stay in and a good meal," the man wrote. Polkinghorne accepted the invitation and led an engaging discussion with the group. He stayed in the man's home that night, and just before heading to the train station to return to Cambridge, the man handed him an envelope. The group had taken up a collection to pay Polkinghorne an honorarium. Polkinghorne opened the envelope, took out the exact amount for his train fare, and returned the balance.

For this final event at the God and Physics conference, he reflected on bottom-up thinking with this eager audience for more than an hour. "With both science and religion, you start in the basement of experience, rather than on the tenth floor and work your way down," he said.

When he finished, the sustained ovation spoke for both the talk he had just given, and also for the lifetime of illumination he has provided.

Lord Harries responded to Polkinghorne's talk, referring to the physicist/priest repeatedly as a voice of credibility and sanity. Harries connected the eighty-year-old scholar's work to the sixth-century philosopher Boethius, who wrote,

> *What binds all things to order,*
> *Governing earth and sea and sky,*
> *Is love…*
> *O happy race of men,*
> *If the love that rules the stars*
> *May also rule your hearts!*[1]

Polkinghorne believes the future is wide open, waiting to be born, ever revealing the love of God. We catch glimpses of it where we can – sometimes in the cosmos, sometimes in our hearts, sometimes in other people. He is the first to admit that, despite all that's been said and written and discovered, there is more to observe, more experiments to conduct, and more to tell. Right now it's enough to know that the world is rationally transparent and rationally beautiful.

But there's always more to the story.

Acknowledgments

We would like to thank the John Templeton Foundation for a grant that enabled us to work on this book; Point Loma Nazarene University (PLNU) generously awarded Dean Nelson a sabbatical; the Wesleyan Center for 21st Century Studies at PLNU also awarded us an additional grant. We thank Tony Collins at Monarch Books for his enthusiasm in getting this story out; to Chip MacGregor of MacGregor Literary for seeing the promise of this project and connecting us to Monarch; to Doug Fruehling of the Ryan Learning Center at PLNU for his expert research help and for keeping us amused throughout; and to Vanessa Nelson for her administrative assistance.

And we thank John Polkinghorne for setting aside his British reticence and opening up his life to us.

Finally we thank the many people – we think the majority – interested in the pursuit of Truth who want to look at the world through two eyes, instead of one.

Notes

Chapter One

1. Carey Goldberg, "Crossing Flaming Swords Over God and Physics," *The New York Times*, 20 April, 1999.
2. Steven Weinberg, *The First Three Minutes: A Modern View of the Origin of the Universe*, updated ed. (New York: Basic, 1993), 154.
3. Steven Weinberg, *Facing Up: Science and Its Cultural Adversaries* (Cambridge, Mass.; Harvard University Press, 2003), 230.
4. Ibid, 242.
5. Steven Weinberg and John Polkinghorne: An Exchange. "Was the Universe Designed?" http://www.counterbalance.net/cqinterv/swjp-frame.html
6. Ibid.
7. John Hedley Brooke, *Science and Religion: Some Historical Perspectives* (Cambridge: Cambridge University Press, 1991), 2.
8. Christopher Hitchens, *God is Not Great: How Religion Poisons Everything* (New York: Warner Books, 2007), 71.
9. Richard Dawkins, "God's Utility Function," *Scientific American* 273.5 (November 1995): 62–67.
10. Richard Dawkins, *A Devil's Chaplain: Selected Essays by Richard Dawkins* (London: Weidenfeld and Nicolson, 2003), 117.
11. Ibid, 145.
12. Ibid, 117.
13. Ibid, 160–61.
14. H. Allen Orr, "A Passion for Evolution" (review of Dawkins' book *A Devil's Chaplain*) *New York Review of Books* 51.3 (February 26, 2004): 28.
15. Richard Dawkins, *The Ancestor's Tale: A Pilgrimage to the Dawn of Evolution* (Boston: Houghton Mifflin, 2004), 613–14.
16. Karl W. Giberson and Donald A. Yerxa, *Species of Origins: America's Search for a Creation Story* (Lanham, Md.: Rowman and Littlefield, 2002), 119–50.
17. Peter Atkins, *The Creation* (Oxford, UK, Freeman, 1981), vii.
18. Ibid.
19. Michael White and John Gribben, *Stephen Hawking: A Life in Science*, new ed. (Washington: Joseph Henry Press, 2002), 3.
20. Stephen Hawking, *Black Holes and Baby Universes and Other Essays* (New York: Bantam, 1994), 173.
21. Carl Sagan, *Cosmos* TV Series, episode 7, scene 5, "Ancient Greek Scientists."
22. Carl Sagan, *The Demon-Haunted World: Science as a Candle in the Dark* (London: Headline, 1997), 263.
23. Keay Davidson, *Carl Sagan: A Life* (New York: J. Wiley, 1999), 420.
24. Carl Sagan, *Broca's Brain: Reflections on the Romance of Science* (New York: Ballantine, 1980) 332–33.
25. Edward O. Wilson, *Consilience: Unity of Knowledge* (New York: Knopf, 1998), 6.
26. Ibid, 257.
27. Ibid, 262.
28. Edward O. Wilson, *On Human Nature* (Cambridge, Mass.: Harvard University Press, 1978), 201.

29. Stephen Jay Gould, Rocks of Ages: *Science and Religion in the Fullness of Life* (New York: Ballantine, 1999), 4.

30. Weinberg, *The First Three Minutes*, 154.

31. Ibid, 154–55.

32. Weinberg, *Facing Up*, 42–43.

33. Weinberg, *Dreams of a Final Theory*, 241.

34. Ibid, 245–46.

35. Weinberg, *Facing Up*, 239–40.

36. Steven Weinberg and John Polkinghorne: An Exchange.

37. John Horgan, *The End of Science: Facing the Limits of Knowledge in the Twilight of the Scientific Age* (New York: Broadway, 1997), 76.

38. Ibid, 77.

39. Weinberg, *Facing Up*, 242.

40. George Johnson, "A Free-for-All on Science and Religion," *The New York Times*, November 21, 2006.

41. Steven Weinberg and John Polkinghorne: An Exchange.

42. Ibid.

43. Michael Polanyi, *Personal Knowledge: Towards a Post-Critical Philosophy* (Chicago: University of Chicago, 1974), vii.

44. John Polkinghorne, *One World: The Interaction of Faith and Science* (Princeton: Princeton University Press, 1987), 36.

45. Ibid, 42.

46. Steven Weinberg and John Polkinghorne: An Exchange.

Chapter Two

1. John Polkinghorne, *From Physicist to Priest: An Autobiography* (Eugene: Cascade Books, 2007), 10.

2. Ibid, 4.

3. Ibid, 9.

4. Ibid, 27.

5. John Polkinghorne, *Quarks, Chaos and Christianity: Questions to Science and Religion* (New York: Crossroad, 2005), 12.

6. Michael Polanyi, *Personal Knowledge: Towards a Post-Critical Philosophy* (Chicago: University of Chicago Press, 1974), 18.

7. Ibid, 138.

8. Ibid, 143.

9. Ibid, 145.

10. Ibid, 237.

11. Ibid, 301.

12. Ibid, 310.

13. Polkinghorne, *Quarks, Chaos and Christianity*, 47.

14. Francis S. Collins, *The Language of God: A Scientist Presents Evidence For Belief* (New York: Free Press, 2006), 6.

15. Polkinghorne, *Quarks, Chaos and Christianity*, 15.

16. Quoted in Collins, 39.

17. Polkinghorne, *From Physicist to Priest*, 37.

18. Ibid, 64.

19. Ibid, 70.

20. Ibid, 70–71.

21. Ibid, 73.

22. Ibid, 74.

23. Ibid, 76.

24. Ibid, 78.

25. Polkinghorne, *Quarks, Chaos and Christianity*, 10.

26. Polkinghorne, *From Physicist to Priest*, 85.

27. Ibid, 85.

28. Polkinghorne, *Quarks, Chaos and Christianity*, 115.

29. Ibid, 57.

30. Ibid, 61.

31. John Polkinghorne and Nicholas Beale, *Questions of Truth: Fifty-one Responses to Questions about God, Science, and Belief* (Louisville: Westminster John Knox Press, 2009), 16.

32. Polkinghorne, *Quarks, Chaos and Christianity*, 61.

Chapter Three

1. Polkinghorne, *From Physicist to Priest*, 99.
2. Larry Dossey, Herbert Benson, John Polkinghorne, and Others, *Healing Through Prayer: Health Practitioners Tell The Story* (Toronto: Anglican Book Centre, 1999), 24.
3. William J. Cromie, "Prayers don't help heart surgery patients," *Harvard Gazette*, 6 April, 2006, http://www.news.harvard.edu/gazette/2006/04.06/05-prayer.html (accessed August 5, 2010).
4. Zev Chavets, "Is There A Right Way To Pray?" *The New York Times Magazine*, 20 September 20, 2009, 46.
5. Polkinghorne, *From Physicist to Priest*, 85.
6. Collins, 220.
7. David Watson, *Fear No Evil: A Personal Struggle With Cancer* (London: Hodder Christian paperbacks, 1984), 25.
8. Ibid, 57.
9. Fraser Watts, *Perspectives On Prayer* (London: Society for Promoting Christian Knowledge, 2001), 36.
10. John Polkinghorne, *Searching For Truth: Lenten Meditations on Science and Faith* (New York: Crossroad Publishing, 1996), 99.
11. Watts, 27.
12. Ibid, 28.
13. Ibid, 30.
14. Ibid, 29.
15. Ibid, 35.
16. Ibid, 36.
17. Dossy, Benson, Polkinghorne, and Others, 22.
18. John Polkinghorne, *Science and Providence: God's Interaction With The World* (West Conshohocken: Templeton Foundation Press, 2005), 83–84.
19. Polkinghorne, *Searching For Truth*, 108.
20. Watts, 37.
21. Keith Ward, *The Big Questions in Science and Religion* (West Conshohocken: Templeton Foundation Press, 2008), 251.
22. Polkinghorne, *Searching For Truth*, 105.
23. Ibid, 106.
24. Polkinghorne, *From Physicist To Priest*, 172.

Chapter Four

1. John Polkinghorne, *Faith of a Physicist* (Minneapolis: Fortress Press, 1996), 158.
2. John D. Zizioulas, *Being As Communion* (Crestwood, NY, 1985), 115.
3. Ibid.
4. Ibid, 115, 122.
5. Ibid, 120.
6. John Polkinghorne, *Science and the Trinity: The Christian Encounter with Reality* (New Haven: Yale University Press, 2004), 126–38.
7. Polkinghorne, *From Physicist to Priest*, 108.
8. John Polkinghorne, *One World*, 83.
9. Ibid, 84.
10. N. T. Wright, "Can A Scientist Believe in the Resurrection?" *The James Gregory Lecture*, St Andrews, 20 December, 2007, 4.
11. John Polkinghorne, *Science and Theology: An Introduction* (Minneapolis: Fortress Press, 1998), 103.
12. Ibid, 104.
13. Ibid, 106
14. Ibid, 107.
15. John Polkinghorne, *Scientists As Theologians: A Comparison of the Writings of Ian Barbour, Arthur Peacocke and John Polkinghorne* (London: Society for Promoting Christian Knowledge, 1996), 77.
16. Polkinghorne, *Science and*

Theology, 92.

17. Ibid, 121.

18. Ibid, 121–22.

19. Polkinghorne, *Science and Theology*, 92.

20. Polkinghorne, *Science and Providence*, 53.

21. Ibid, 59–63.

22. Polkinghorne, *Science and Theology*, 93.

23. Polkinghorne, *Scientists as Theologians*, 41.

24. N.T. Wright, 10.

25. Ibid, 11.

Chapter Five

1. Quoted in Rodney D. Holder, "Is the Universe Designed?" *The Faraday Papers*, No. 10, April, 2007.

2. Polkinghorne, *Quarks, Chaos and Christianity*, 37–40.

3. Polkinghorne, *Science and Providence*, 26.

4. Polkinghorne and Beale, 44.

5. Ibid, 102.

6. Quoted in Polkinghorne, *Faith of a Physicist*, 76

7. John Polkinghorne, *Traffic in Truth: Exchanges Between Science and Theology* (Minneapolis: Fortress Press, 2002), 33–34.

8. Ibid, 35.

9. Polkinghorne, *Quarks, Chaos and Christianity*, 43.

10. Ibid, 36.

11. Ibid, 37.

12. Quoted in Paul Davies, *Cosmic Jackpot: Why Our Universe is Just Right for Life* (New York: Houghton Mifflin, 2007), 222.

13. Polkinghorne, *Quarks, Chaos and Christianity*, 47.

14. Ibid, 52.

15. Polkinghorne, *Science and the Trinity*, 66.

16. Ibid, 68.

17. John Polkinghorne, *Faith, Science and Understanding* (New Haven:

Yale University Press, 2000), 22.

18. Polkinghorne, *One World*, 80.

19. Polkinghorne, *Science and Providence*, 46–47.

20. Ibid, 51.

21. John Polkinghorne, ed., *The Work of Love: Creation as Kenosis* (Grand Rapids: William B. Eerdmans, 2001), 94.

22. Ibid.

23. Ibid, 102.

24. Polkinghorne, *Traffic in Truth*, 17.

25. Polkinghorne, *Faith of a Physicist*, 81.

26. Polkinghorne, *Science and the Trinity*, 81.

27. Ibid, 65.

Chapter Six

1. John Polkinghorne, *Exploring Reality: The Intertwining of Science and Religion* (New Haven: Yale University Press, 2005), 154.

2. Polkinghorne, *From Physicist to Priest*, 167.

3. Polkinghorne, *Exploring Reality*, 147.

4. John Polkinghorne, *Belief in God in an Age of Science* (New Haven: Yale University Press, 1998), 93.

5. Polkinghorne, *Exploring Reality*, 152.

6. Ibid, 153–54.

7. Ibid, 54.

8. Quoted in Thomas Jay Oord, ed., *John Polkinghorne Reader* (unpublished manuscript) 66–67.

9. Ibid.

10. Polkinghorne, *Faith of a Physicist*, 153.

11. Oord, 67.

12. Polkinghorne, *Faith, Science and Understanding*, 37.

13. Polkinghorne, *Quarks, Chaos and Christianity*, 63.

14. Polkinghorne, *Faith, Science and Understanding*, 109.

15. Ibid, 55.

Chapter Seven

1. John Polkinghorne, *Living with Hope: A Scientists Looks At Advent, Christmas, and Epiphany* (Louisville: Westminster John Knox Press, 2003), 45.
2. John Polkinghorne, *The God of Hope and the End of the World* (New Haven: Yale University Press, 2002), 106.
3. Ward, *The Big Questions in Science And Religion*, 161.
4. Polkinghorne, *Science and the Trinity*, 161.
5. Polkinghorne, *The God of Hope and the End of the World*, 107.
6. Ibid, 113.
7. Ibid.
8. Polkinghorne and Beale, *Questions of Truth*, 22.
9. Polkinghorne, *The God of Hope and the End of The World*, 116.
10. Ibid, 35.
11. Ibid.
12. Ibid, 36.
13. Ibid, xvii.
14. Ibid, 21.
15. Ibid, 44.
16. Ibid, 99.
17. Ibid, 115.
18. Polkinghorne, *Searching For Truth*, 133.
19. Polkinghorne, *The God of Hope and the End of the World*, 126.
20. Ibid, 127–28.
21. Ibid, 132.
22. Ibid, 128.
23. C. S. Lewis, *The Great Divorce* (New York: MacMillan Publishing, 1946), 72.
24. Polkinghorne, *Faith of a Physicist*, 171.
25. Polkinghorne, *Living with Hope*, 58.
26. Ibid.
27. Ibid, 59.
28. Polkinghorne, *Faith of a Physicist*, 172.
29. Polkinghorne, *Exploring Reality*, 174.
30. John Polkinghorne, and Michael Welker eds, *The End of the World and the Ends of God* (Harrosburg: Trinity Press International, 2000), 7.
31. Ibid, 12.
32. Ibid.
33. Quoted in Polkinghorne and Welker, *The End of the World and the Ends of God*, 252.
34. Ibid, 276.
35. Ibid, 30.
36. Ibid, 39.
37. Polkinghorne and Beale, *Questions of Truth*, 23.
38. Polkinghorne, *Faith of a Physicist*, 164 and 168.
39. Ibid, 170.
40. Quoted in Ward, 143.
41. Polkinghorne and Welker, *The Ends of the World and the Ends of God*, 32.
42. Ibid.
43. Polkinghorne and Beale, *Questions of Truth*, 24.
44. Ward, 161.
45. Polkinghorne, *Science and the Trinity*, 180.
46. Ibid, 150–51.
47. Ibid, 159.
48. Polkinghorne, *Faith of a Physicist*, 163.
49. Ibid, 164.
50. Quoted in Polkinghorne, *Faith of a Physicist,* 164.

Chapter Eight

1. John Polkinghorne, *The Way the World Is: The Christian Perspective of a Scientist* (Louisville: Westminster John Knox Press, 2007), vii.
2. Ibid, ix.
3. Polkinghorne, *Quarks, Chaos and Christianity*, 115.
4. Polkinghorne, *The Way the World Is*, 5.

5. John Polkinghorne, *Quantum Physics and Theology: An Unexpected Kinship* (New Haven: Yale University Press, 2007), 109–10.
6. Polkinghorne, *The Way the World Is*, 112.
7. Ibid.
8. Ibid, 112–13.
9. Ibid, 104.
10. Ibid, 105.
11. Ibid, 105–106.
12. Ibid, 106.
13. Ibid.
14. Polkinghorne, *Science and the Trinity*, 175.
15. Ibid.
16. Polkinghorne, *Exploring Reality*, 128.
17. Polkinghorne, *Faith of a Physicist*, 177.
18. Polkinghorne, *Exploring Reality*, 127.
19. Polkinghorne, *Faith of a Physicist*, 182.
20. Ibid, 183.
21. Ibid.
22. Ibid, 184.
23. Ibid, 185.
24. Ibid.
25. Ibid, 189.
26. Ibid, 191.
27. Ibid.
28. Polkinghorne, *Science and the Trinity*, 176.
29. Polkinghorne, *Exploring Reality*, 133.
30. Polkinghorne, *Science and the Trinity*, 177.
31. Polkinghorne, *The God of Hope and the End of the World*, 120–27.
32. Polkinghorne, *Exploring Reality*, 128.
33. Ibid, 129.
34. Ibid, 130.
35. Ibid, 131.
36. Polkinghorne, *Faith of a Physicist*, 179.
37. Ibid, 180–81.
38. Polkinghorne, *Belief in God in an Age of Science*, 110.
39. Polkinghorne, *Exploring Reality*, 135.
40. Polkinghorne, *The Way the World Is*, 108.
41. Ibid, 110–11.
42. Polkinghorne, *Science and the Trinity*, 177–78.
43. Ibid, 178 and 180.
44. Polkinghorne and Beale, *Questions of Truth*, 69–70.
45. Ibid, 97.
46. Polkinghorne, *Quantum Physics and Theology*, 95.
47. John Polkinghorne, *Quantum Theory: A Very Short Introduction* (Oxford: Oxford University Press, 2002), 87.
48. Ibid, 56.
49. Polkinghorne, *Quantum Physics and Theology*, 91.

Epilogue

1. Boethius, *The Theological Tractates*, (Cambridge, Mass.: Harvard University Press, 1973), 227.